# Spiritually Speaking and Walking

# With the Word of God

## ( A Years Journey )

By : Patricia A . Jacobs

I

# Copyright

Published by Patricia A .C .  Jacobs
© 2014 , Patricia A.C. Jacobs

ISBN 978 - 0 - 9815658 - 4-2
ISBN        0 - 9815658 - 4-0


First Edition
First Printing , May 2014
1 0 9 8 7 6 5 4 3 2 1

Scriptures are taken from The King James Version of the Bible


Printed in the United States of America

# Table of Contents

# Introduction

Spiritually Speaking and Walking with the Word of God (A Years Journey) , all started when I was given a daily planner . As I pondered within myself as to what I would do with it , my conclusion was to continue to record Gods words as I received it daily . Some scriptures continued to speak to my heart over and over again and it always seemed to impact me with greater faith , hope , trust and strength in the Lord . Most of my traveled journeys have been in The Book of Psalms and through other Books of the Bible as well . As you begin your journey I know you will gain a greater hunger and thirst after the true and living word of God .

May God Bless You and Yours

# Spiritually Speaking and

# Walking With the Word of God

( A Years Journey )

By : Patricia A. Jacobs

# January 1

Proverbs 7 : 1 - 4

(1)My son , keep my words , and lay up my commandments with thee.

(2) Keep my commandments , and live ; and my law as the apple of thine eye.

(3)Bind them upon thy fingers , write them upon the table of thine heart .

(4) Say unto wisdom , Thou art my sister ; and call understanding thy kinswoman ;

Psalm 11: 1

In the Lord put I my trust ; how say ye to my soul ,Flee as a bird to your mountain ?

# January 2

Isaiah 59 : 4

None calleth for justice , nor any pleaded for truth ; they trust in vanity , and speak lies ; they conceive mischief , and bring forth iniquity .

Isaiah 60 : 1-2

(1)Arise , shine; for thy light is come , and the glory of the Lord is risen upon thee.

(2) For, behold , the darkness shall cover the earth ;and gross darkness the people; but the Lord shall arise upon thee and his glory shall be seen upon thee.

1 Kings 8 : 1

Then Solomon assembled the elders of Israel , and all the heads of the tribes , the chief of the fathers of the children of Israel, that they might bring up the ark of the covenant of the Lord out of the city of David , which is Zion .

Psalm 85 : 1

Lord , thou hast been favorable unto thy land ; thou hast brought back the captivity of Jacob.

## January 3

Ecclesiastes 10 : 10

If the iron be blunt , and he do not whet the edge , then must he put to more strength ; but wisdom is profitable to direct.

Ecclesiastes 11 : 4

He that observeth the wind shall not sow; and he that regarded the clouds shall not reap.

Psalm 70 : 1

Make haste , O God , to deliver me; make haste to help me , O Lord.

Psalm 71 : 1

In the , O Lord , do I put my trust; let me never be put to confusion.

Psalm 128 : 2

For thou shalt  eat the labour of thine hands ; happy shalt thou be, and it shall be well with thee.

Psalm 131 : 1

Lord , my heart is not haunty, nor mine eyes lofty; neither do I exercise myself in great matters ,or in things too high for me.

Psalm 135 : 4-6

(4) For the Lord hath chosen Jacob unto himself , and Israel for his peculiar treasure.

(5) For I know that the Lord is great, and that our Lord is above all gods.

(6) Whatsoever the Lord pleased , that did he in Heaven, and in earth, in the seas , and all deep places.

## January 4

Psalm 135 : 1
Praise ye the Lord . Praise ye the name of the Lord ; praise him ,
O ye servants of the Lord.

## January 5

Job 39 : 6
Whose house I have made the wilderness, and the barren lands
his dwelling.
Psalm 31: 14
But I trusted in thee , O Lord : I said , Thou art my God.
Psalm 128 :2
For thou shall eat the labour of thine hands : happy shall thou be
, and it shall be well with thee.
Job 39 : 1-2
(1)Knowest thou the time when the wild goats of the rock bring
forth ? Or canst thou mark when the hinds do calve?
(2)Canst thou number the months that they fulfill ? Or knowest
thou the time when they bring forth?
Psalm 48 : 1
Great is the Lord , and greatly to be praised in the city of our
God , in the mountain of his holiness .

## January 6

Joel 2 : 23-32
(23)Be glad then , ye children of Zion ;for he hath given
you the former rain moderately , and he will cause to
come down for you the rain  , the former rain , and the

(24)And the floors shall be full of wheat , and the fats
shall overflow with wine and oil.
(25)And I will restore to you the years that the locust hath eaten ,
the cankerworm , and the caterpillar , and the palmerworm , my
great army which I sent among you .
(26)And ye shall eat in plenty and be satisfied , and praise the
name of the Lord your God , that hath dealt wondrously with
you : and my people shall never be ashamed.
(27)And ye shall know that I am in the mist of Israel , and that I
am the Lord your God , and none else : and my people shall
never be ashamed .
(28)And it shall come to pass afterward , that I will pour out my
spirit upon all flesh ; and your sons and your daughters shall
prophesy , your old men shall dream dreams , your young men
shall see visions :
(29) And also upon the servants and upon the handmaids in
those days will I pour out my spirit .
(30)And I show wonders in the heavens and in the earth , blood ,
and fire , and pillars of smoke.
(31) The sun shall be turned into darkness , and the moon into
blood , before the great and the terrible day of the Lord come.
(32)And it shall come to pass , that whosoever shall call on the
name of the Lord shall be delivered : for in mount Zion and in
Jerusalem shall be deliverance , as the Lord hath said , and in the
remnant whom the Lord shall call.
Joel 3 : 1
For , behold , in those days , and in that time , when I shall bring
again the captivity of Judah  and Jerusalem .
Psalm 31 : 14
But I trusted in thee , O Lord :I said , Thou art my God.

## January 7

Psalm 77 : 17 - 20

(17)The clouds poured out water : the skies sent out a sound : thine arrows also went abroad .

(18) The voice of thy thunder was in the heaven : the earth lightings lightened the world : the earth trembled and shook .

(19) Thy way is in the sea , and thy footsteps are not known.

(20) Thou leadest the people like a flock by the hand of Moses and Aaron.

Psalm 78 : 46

He gave also their increase unto the caterpillar , and their labour unto the locust.

Psalm 89 : 8

O Lord God of hosts , who is a strong Lord like unto thee? Or to thy faithfulness round about thee?

Psalm 17 : 13-15

(13) Arise , O Lord , disappoint him , cas him down : deliver my soul from the wicked , which is thy sword :

(14) From men which are thy hand , O Lord , from men of the world , which have their portion in this life , and whose belly thou fillest with thy hid treasure : they are full of children , and leave the rest of their substance to their babes.

(15) As for me . I will behold thy face in righteousness : I shall be satisfied , when I awake , with thy likeness .

## January 8

Psalm 31 : 17

Let me not be ashamed , O Lord : for I have called upon thee , let the wicked be ashamed , and let them be silent in the grave.

Psalm 31 : 14

But I trusted in thee , O Lord : I said , Thou art my God.

Psalm 31 : 15

My times are in thy hand : deliver me from the hand of mine enemies , and from them that persecute me.

Psalm 29 :11

The LORD will give strength unto his people ; the LORD will bless his people with peace .

## January 9

Psalm 135 : 4-6

(4)For the Lord hath chosen Jacob unto himself , and Israel for his peculiar treasure.

(5) For I know that the Lord is great , and that our Lord is above all gods.

(6)Whatsoever he Lord pleased , that did he in heaven , and in earth , in the seas , and all deep places.

Acts 17 : 24-28

(24) God that made the world and all things therein , seeing that he is Lord of heaven and earth , dwellth not in temples made with hands ;

(25) Neither is worshipped with men's hands , as though he needed any thing , seeing he giveth to all life , and breath , and all things ;

(26) And hath made of one blood all nations of men for to dwell on all the face of the earth , and hath determined the times before appointed , and the bounds of their habitation:

(27) That they should seek the Lord , if haply they might feel after him , and find him , though he be not far from every one of us:

(28)For in him we live , and move , and have our being ; as certain also of your own poets have said , For we are also his offspring.

## January 10

Jeremiah 32 : 42
For thus saith the Lord ; Like evil upon this people , so will I bring upon them all the good that I have promised them .
Psalm 128 : 2
For thou shalt eat the labour of thine hands : happy shalt thou be , and it shall be well with thee.
Psalm 65:11
Thou crownest the year with thy goodness : and thy paths drop fatness.
Psalm 66 :1
To the chief Musician , A Song or Psalm .Make a joyful noise unto God , all ye lands:

## January 11

Psalm 68 :14-15
(14)When the Almighty scattered kings in it , it was white as snow in Sal'-mon .
(15)The hill of God is as the hill of Ba'-shan : an high hill as the hill of Ba'-shan.
Psalm 129:1
Many a time have they afflicted me from my youth ,may Israel now say:
Proverbs 4:5
Get wisdom , get understanding : forget it not ; neither decline from the words of my mouth.

## January 12

Psalm 80 : 15-19

(15) And the vineyard which thy right hand hath planted , and the branch that thou madest strong for thyself.

(16) It is burned with fire , it is cut down : they perish at the rebuke of thy countenance.

(17) Let thy hand be upon the man of thy right hand ,upon the son of man whom thou madest strong for thyself.

(18) So will not we go back from thee : quicken us ,and we will call upon thy name.

(19) Turn us again , O Lord God of hosts, cause thy face to shine : and we shall be saved.

Psalm 80 :14

Return , we beseech thee , O God of hosts : look down from heaven , and behold , and visit this vine;

## January 13

Isaiah 22 : 21-25

(21) I will clothe him with thy robe , and strengthen him with thy girdle , and I will commit thy government into his hand : and he shall be a father to the inhabitants of Jerusalem , and to the house of Judah.

(22) And the key of the house of David will I lay upon his shoulder ; so he shall open, and none shall shut , and none shall open .

(23) And I will fasten him as a nail in a sure place : and he shall be for a glorious throne to his father's house.

(24) And they shall hang upon him all the glory of his father's house , the offspring and the issue , all vessels of small

quantity , from the vessels of cups , even to all the vessels of flagons .

(25) In that day , saith the Lord of hosts , shall the nail that is fastened in the sure place be removed , and be cut off: for the Lord hath spoken it .

Psalm 148 : 2

Praise ye him , all his angels : praise ye him , all his hosts.

Proverbs 1:5

A wise man will hear , and will increase learning : and a man of understanding shall attain unto wise counsels:

Psalm 77:11

I will remember the works of the Lord : surely I will remember thy wonders of old .

## January 14

Psalm 78: 42

They remembered not his hand , nor the day when he delivered them from the enemy.

Psalm 78:41

Yea , they turned back and tempted God , and limited the Holy One of Israel.

Psalm 107:22

And let them sacrifice the sacrifices of thanksgiving , and declare his works with rejoicing.

Psalm 81:7

Thou calledst in trouble , and I delivered thee : I answered thee in the secret place of thunder : I proved thee at the waters of Mer'-I-bah .Selah.

Psalm 85:1

Lord , thou hast been favorable unto thy land ; thou hast brought back the captivity of Jacob.

## January 15

Psalm 102 :1
Hear my prayer , O Lord  ,  and let my cry come unto thee .
Psalm 101 : 6
Praise ye the Lord . O give thanks unto the Lord ; for he is good ; for his mercy endureth for ever.
Psalm 97 : 1
The Lord reigneth ; let the earth rejoice ; let the multitude of isles be glad thereof.

## January 16

Psalm 101 : 6
Praise ye the Lord ; O give thanks unto the Lord ; for he is good : for his mercy endureth for ever.
Psalm 7 : 9
Oh let the wickedness of the wicked come to an end ; but establish the just : for the righteous God trieth the hearts and reins .

## January 17

Psalm 27 : 7
Hear , O Lord , when I cry with my voice : have mercy
also upon me ,and answer me .
Malachi 3 : 6
For I am the Lord , I change not ; therefore ye sons of Jacob are not consumed.

## January 18

Psalm 139 : 23-24
(23) Search me O God and know my heart : try me , and know my thoughts:

(24) And see if there be any wicked way in me , and lead me in the way everlasting.

Psalm 141 : 1-2

(1) Lord , I cry unto thee : make haste unto me ; give ear unto my voice , when I cry unto thee .

(2) Let my prayer be set forth before thee as incense , and the lifting up of my hands as the evening sacrifice.

Psalm 140 : 1

Deliver me , O Lord , from the evil man : preserve me from the violent man:

## January 19

Psalm 96 : 10-11

(10)Say among the heathen that the Lord reigneth ; the world also shall be established that it shall not be moved : he shall judge the people righteously.

(11) Let the heavens rejoice , and let the earth be glad ;
let the sea roar , and the fullness therefore.

Proverbs 7 : 1-6

(1) My son , keep my words , and lay up my commandments with thee .

(2) Keep my commandments , and live ; and my law as
the apple of thine eye.

(3) Bind them upon thy fingers , write them upon the table of thine heart .

(4) Sat unto wisdom , Thou art my sister ; and call understanding thy kinswoman :

(5) That they may keep thee from the strange woman , from the stranger which flattereth with her words.

(6) For at the window of my house I looked through my casement,

## January 20

Psalm 104 : 31

The glory of the Lord shall endure for ever ; the Lord shall rejoice in his works.

Psalm 119 : 105

Thy word is a lamp unto my feet , and a light unto my path .

Psalm 119 : 157

Many are my persecutors and mine enemies ; yet do I not decline from thy testimonies.

Psalm 119 : 137

Righteous art thou , O Lord , and upright are thy judgments .

Psalm 119 : 145

I cried with my whole heart ; hear me . O Lord : I will keep thy statutes.

## January 21

Proverbs 15 : 30

The light of the eyes rejoiceth the heart : and a good report maketh the bones fat .

Psalm 143 : 7

Hear me speedily , O Lord : my spirit faileth : hide not thy face from me ,lest I be like unto them that go down into the pit .

Psalm 143 : 8

Cause me to hear thy loving kindness in the morning ; for in thee do I trust ; cause me to know the way wherein I should walk ; for I lift up my soul unto thee.

Jeremiah  14 : 4-5

(4) Because the ground is chapt , for there was no rain in the earth , the plowmen were ashamed , they covered their heads.
(5)Yea ,the hind also calved in the field , and forsook it , because there was no grass.

Jeremiah 14 : 15

Therefore thus saith the Lord concerning the prophets that prophesy in my name , and I sent them not , yet they say , Sword and famine shall not be in this land : By sword and famine shall those prophets be consumed .

Psalm 128 : 2

For thou shall eat the labour of thine hands ; happy shalt thou be , and it shall be as a fruitful vine by the sides of thine house : house about thy table .

## January 22

Psalm 1 : 1-3

(1) Blessed is the man that walketh not in the counsel of the ungodly , nor standeth in the way of sinners , nor sitteth in the seat of the scornful .

(2) But his light is in the law of the Lord ; and in his law doth he meditate day and night.

Psalm 37 : 34

Wait on the Lord , and keep his way , and he shall exalt thee to inherit the land ; when the wicked are cut off , thou shalt see it.

## January 23

Psalm 85 : 1

Lord , thou hast been favorable unto thy land : thou hast brought back the captivity of Jacob.

2 Chronicles 2 : 4

Behold , I build an house to the name of the Lord my God , to dedicate it to him , and to burn before him sweet incense , and for the continual shewbread , and for the burnt offerings morning and evening on the Sabbaths , and on the new moons , and on the solemn feasts of the Lord our God. This is an ordinance foe ever to Israel .

Psalm 40 : 1

I waited patiently for the lord ; and he inclined unto me , and heard my cry.

## January 24

Jeremiah 14 : 4-5

(4 ) Because the ground is chapt , for there was no rain in the earth , the plowmen were ashamed , they covered their heads.
(5) Yea , the hind also calved in the field , and forsook it , because there was no grass.

Jeremiah 14 : 14

Then the Lord said unto me , The prophets prophesy lies in my name : I sent the not ,neither have I commanded them, neither spake unto them : they prophesy unto you a false vision and divination , and a thing of nought , and the deceit of their heart.

Psalm 128 : 2

For thou shalt eat the labour of thine hands ; happy shalt thou be , and it shall be well with thee.

Psalm 86 : 4-5

(4) Rejoice the soul of thy servant : for unto thee , O Lord , do I lift up my soul .
(5) For thou , Lord , art good , and ready to forgive ; and plenteous in mercy unto all them that call upon thee.

## January 25

Psalm 89 : 11

The heavens are thine , the earth also is thine : as for the world and the fulness thereof , thou hast founded them .

## January 26

Psalm 143 : 4-8
(4) Therefore is my spirit overwhelmed within me ; my heart within me is desolate .
(5) I remember the days of old ; I meditate on all thy works , I muse on the work of thy hands .
(6) I stretch forth my hands unto thee , my soul thirsteth after thee , as a thirsty land . Selah .
(7) Hear me speedily , O Lord : my spirit faileth ; hide not thy face from me , lest I be like unto them that go down into the pit .
(8) Cause me to hear thy lovingkindness in the morning ; for in thee do I put my trust : cause me to know the way
wherein I should walk ; for I lift up my soul unto thee.
Acts 2 : 25 -27
(25) For David speaketh concerning him , I foresaw the Lord always before my face ,
for he is on my right hand , that I should not be moved :
(26) Therefore did my hart rejoice , and my tongue was glad ; moreover also my flesh shall rest in hope :
(27) Because thou will not leave my soul in hell , neither wilt thou suffer thine Holy One to see corruption .
Psalm 104 : 28
That thou givest them they gather : thou openest thine hand , they are filled with good .

## January 27

Psalm 20 : 1
The Lord hear thee in the day of trouble ; the name of the God of Jacob defend thee:
Psalm 22 :24
For he hath not despised nor abhorred the affliction of the afflicted ; neither hath he hid his face from him ; but when he

cried unto him , he heard .
Psalm 22 : 31
They shall come , and shall declare hi righteousness unto a
people that shall be born , that he hath done this.
Joel 2 : 23-27
(23) Be glad then , ye children of Zion , and rejoice in the Lord
your God : for he hath given you the former rain moderately ,
and he will cause to come down for you the rain , the former rain
, and the latter rain in the first month.
(24) And the floors shall be full of wheat , and the vats shall
overflow with wine and oil .
(25) And I will restore to you the years that the locust hath eaten
, the cankerworm , and the caterpillar , and the palmerworm ,
my great army which I sent among you.
(26) And ye shall eat in plenty , and be satisfied , and praise the
name of the Lord your God , that hath dealt wondrously with
you : and my people shall never be ashamed
(27) And ye shall know that I am in the midst of Israel , and none
else : and my people shall never be ashamed .

## January 28

Psalm 85 : 1
Lord , thou hast been favorable unto thy land : thou hast brought
back the captivity of Jacob.
Psalm 85 : 7
Show us thy mercy , O Lord , and grant us thy salvation.
Isaiah 60 : 13
The glory of Lebanon shall come unto thee, the fir tree, the pine
tree, and the box together , to beauty the place of my sanctuary ;
and I will make the place of my feet glorious.

## January 29

Nehemiah 4 :1
But it came to pass, that when Sanballat heard that we builded the wall , he was wroth ,and took great indignation , and mocked the Jews.
Nehemiah 4 : 4
Hear , O our God ; for we are despised : and turn their reproach upon their own head , and give them for a prey in the land of captivity :
Psalm 128 : 2
For thou shalt eat the labour of thine hands : happy shalt thou be , and it shall be well with thee.
Psalm 116 :13
I will take the cup of salvation , and call upon the name of the Lord.
Psalm 116 : 14
I will pay my vows unto the Lord now in the presence of his people.

## January 30

Psalm 117 : 1
O Praise the Lord , all ye nations : praise him , all ye people.
Psalm 104 : 27- 28
(27)These wait all upon thee: that thou mayest give them their meat in  due season .
(28) That thou givest them they gather : thou openest thine hand , they are filled with good.

## January 31

Psalm 106 : 4
Remember me , O Lord , with the favour that thou bearest unto

thy people: O visit me with thy salvation;

Nehemiah 6: 12-15

(12) And, lo , I perceived that God had not sent him: but that he pronounced this prophecy against me: for Tobiah and Sanballat had hired .

(13)Therefore was he hired , that I should be afraid , and do so , and sin , and that they might have matter for an evil report , that they might reproach me .

 (14)My God , think thou upon Tobiah and Sanballat according to these their works , and on the prophetess Noadiah , and the rest of the prophets, that would have put me in fear.

(15) So the wall was finished in the twenty and fifth day of the month Elul , in fifty and two days.

Nehemiah 7 : 5

And my God put into thine heart to gather together the nobles , and the rulers , and the people , that they might be reckoned by genealogy. And I found a register of the genealogy of them which came up at the first , and found written therein,

Psalm 22:24

For he hath not despised nor abhorred the afflicted ; neither hath he hid his face from him ; but when he cried unto him , he heard.

## February 1

Psalm 68 : 20- 24
(20) He that is our god is the god of salvation; and unto god the lord belong the issues from death.
(21) But God shall wound the head of his enemies , and the hairy scalp of such an one as goeth on still in his trespasses.
(22) The Lord said, I will bring again from Bashan , I will bring my people again from the depths of the sea:
(23)That thy foot may be dipped in the blood of thine enemies , and the tongue of thy dogs in the same.
(24) They have seen thy goings , O God ; even the goings of my God ; my King , in the sanctuary.
Psalm 68:29
Because of thy temple at Jerusalem shall kings bring presents unto thee.
Psalm 68:19
Blessed be the Lord , who daily loadeth us with benefits , even the God of our salvation. Selah
Psalm 128 : 2
For thou shalt eat the labour of thine hands : happy shalt thou be , and it shall be well with thee.

## February 2

Psalm 135 : 4-6
(4)For the Lord hath chosen Jacob unto himself , and Israel for his peculiar treasure .
(5)For I know that the Lord is great , and that our Lord is above all gods.
(6) Whatsoever the Lord pleased , that did he in heaven, and in earth , in the seas , and all deep places.

Psalm 101 : 6

Mine eyes shall be upon the faithful of the land , that they may dwell with me : he that walketh in a perfect way , he shall serve me.

## February 3

Psalm 96 : 10-11

(10)Say among the heathen that the Lord reigneth : the world also shall be established that I shall not be moved : he shall judge the people righteously.
(11)Let Let the heavens rejoice , and let the earth be glad ; let the sea roar , and the fulness thereof.

1 Kings 20-28

And there came a man of God , and spake unto the king of Israel , and said , Thus saith the Lord , Because the Syrians have said , The Lord is God of the hills , but he is not God of the valleys , therefore will I deliver all this great multitude into thine hand , and ye shall know that I am the Lord .

## February 4

Psalm 40 : 1

To the chief Musician , A Psalm of David . I waited patiently for the Lord; and he inclined unto me , and heard my cry.

Psalm 91 : 1

He that dwelleth in the secret place of the most High shall abide under the shadow of the Almighty.

## February 5

Psalm 89:28

My mercy will I keep for evermore, and my covenant shall stand fast with him.

Psalm 8:6
Thou madest him to have dominion over the works of thy hands
: thou hast put all things under his feet:

## February 6

Psalm 11:4
The Lord is in his holy temple , the LORD'S
throne is in heaven ; his eyes behold , his eyelids try , the
children of men.
Psalm 12 :1
To the chief Musician upon Sheminith , A Psalm of David. Help ,
Lord ; for the godly man ceaseth ; for the faithful fail from among
the children of men.
Psalm 11:1
To the chief Musician , A Psalm of David . In the Lord put I my
trust : how say ye to my soul , Flee as a bird to your mountain?
Psalm 8:9
O LORD our Lord , how excellent is thy name in all the earth!

## February 7

Psalm 4:1
To the chief Musician on Neginoth , A Psalm of David . Hear me
when I call , O God of my righteousness: thou hast enlarged me
when I was in distress ; have mercy upon me , and hear my
prayer.
Psalm 116:13-14
(13)I will take the cup of salvation , and call upon the name of
the Lord.
(14)I will pay my vows unto the Lord now in the presence of all
his people.

Psalm 104:27

These wait all upon thee ; that thou mayest give them their meat in due season.

## February 8

Isaiah 6:8

Also I heard the voice of the Lord , saying , Whom shall I send , and who will go for us ? Then said I , Here am I ; send me.

Amos 1:9

Thus saith the LORD : For three transgressions of Tyrus , and for four , I will not turn away the punishment thereof ; because they delivered up the whole captivity to Edom , and remembered not the brotherly covenant :

Job 8:7

Though thy beginning was small , yet thy latter end should greatly increase .

## February 9

Psalm 31: 24

Be of good courage , and he shall strengthen your heart , all ye that hope in the LORD.

Psalm 32: 1

A Psalm of David , Maschil. Blessed is he whose transgression is forgiven , whose sin is covered.

Psalm 104 : 27

These wait all upon thee; that thou mayest give them their meat in due season .

## February 10

Psalm 89: 14-15

(14)Justice and judgment are the habitation of thy throne : mercy and truth shall go before thy face.

(15)Blessed is the people that know the joyful sound: they shall walk , O LORD , in the light of thy countenance.

Psalm 31:24

Be of good courage , and he shall strengthen your heart , all ye that hope in the LORD.

## February 11

Jeremiah 4:9

And it shall come to pass at that day , saith the LORD , that the heart of the king shall perish , and the heart of the princes ; and the priest shall be astonished , and the prophets shall wonder.

Jeremiah 50: 1-2

(1)The word that the LORD spake against Babylon and against the land of the Chaldeans by Jeremiah the prophet.

(2)Declare ye among the nations , and publish , and set up a standard ; publish , and conceal not : say , Babylon is taken , Bel is confounded, Merodach is broken in pieces ; her idols are confounded , her images are broken in pieces.

Psalm 104:28

That thou givest them they gather : thou openest thine hand , they are filled with good.

Samuel 1:4

And when the time was that Elkanah offered
, he gave to Peninnah his wife , and to all her sons and her daughters , portions:

## February 12

Psalm 65 :9

Thou visitest the earth , and waterest it : thou greatly enriches it with the river of God  , which is full of water : thou preparest them corn , when thou hast so provided for it .

Job 39:17

Because God hath deprived her of wisdom , neither hath he imparted to her understanding .

Psalm 84:12

O LORD of hosts, blessed is the man that trusteth in thee.

## February 13

Psalm 66:1

To the chief Musician , A Song or Psalm . Make a joyful noise unto God , all ye lands:

Psalm 68:19

Blessed be the Lord , who daily loadeth us with benefits , even the God of our salvation. Selah

Isaiah 59: 4

None calleth for justice , nor any pleaded for truth : they trust in vanity , and speak lies ; they conceive mischief, and bring forth iniquity.

Isaiah 60:21

Thy people also shall be all righteous : they shall inherit the land for ever , the work of my hands, that I may be glorified.

## February 14

Psalm 48:13-14

(13)Mark ye well her bulwarks , consider her palaces ; that ye may tell it to the generation following .

(14)For this God is our God for ever and ever: he will be our guide even unto death.

Psalm 119:105

NUN. Thy word is a lamp unto my feet , and a light unto my path.

## February 15

Psalm 119:105

NUN. Thy word is a lamp unto my feet , and a light unto my path.

Psalm 119:161-162

(161)SCHIN . Princes have persecuted me without a cause : but my heart standeth in awe of thy word.

(162)I rejoice at thy word , as one that findeth great spoil.

Psalm 119:160

Thy word is true from the beginning : and every one of thy righteous judgments endureth forever.

Isaiah 48:20

Go ye forth of Babylon , flee ye from the Chileans , with a voice of singing declare ye , tell this , utter it even to the end of the earth ; say ye , The LORD hath redeemed his servant Jacob.

## February 16

Psalm 78: 1-4

(1)Maschil of ASAP . Give ear , O my people , to my law : incline your ears to the words of my mouth.

(2)I will open my mouth in a parable : I will utter dark sayings of old:

(3)Which we have heard and known , and our fathers have told us.

(4)We will not hide them from their children , shewing to the generation to come the praises of the LORD , and his strength , and his wonderful works that he hath done.

Psalm 78:12

Marvellous things did he in the sight of their fathers, in the land of Egypt , in the field of Zoan.

## February 17

Psalm 77:13

Thy way , O God , is in the sanctuary : who is so great a God as our God ?

Psalm 78:48

He gave up their cattle also to the hail , and their flocks to hot thunderbolts.

Psalm 78:7

That they might set their hope in God , and not forget the works of God , but keep his commandments :

Psalm 27:4

One thing have I desired of the LORD , that will I seek after ; that I may dwell in the house of the LORD all the days of my life , to behold the beauty of the LORD , and to inquire in his temple.

## February 18

Psalm 32:1-2

(1)A Psalm of David , Maschil . Blessed is he whose transgression is forgiven , whose sin is covered.

(2)Blessed is the man unto whom the LORD imputed not iniquity , and in whose spirit there is no guile.

Psalm 78:1

Maschil of ASAP . Give ear , O my people , to my law : incline your ears to the words of my mouth.

## February 19

Psalm 37:25

I have been young , and now am old; yet have I have not seen the righteous forsaken , nor his seed begging bread.

Psalm 40:1

To the chief Musician , A Psalm of David . I waited patiently for the LORD ; and he inclined unto me , and hears my cry.

Psalm 119:101-105

(101)I have refrained my feet from every evil way , that I might keep thy word.

(102)I have not departed thy judgments : for thou hast taught me.

(103)How sweet are they words unto my taste ! Yea, sweeter than honey to my mouth!

(104)Through thy percepts I get understanding: therefore I hate every false way.

(105)NUN . Thy word is a lamp unto my feet , and a light unto my path.

## February 20

Psalm 119:157
Many are my persecutors and mine enemies :  yet do I not decline from thy testimonies.

Psalm 119:145
KOPH. I cried with my whole heart : hear me , O LORD : I will keep thy statutes.

Psalm 85:1
To the chief Musician , A Psalm for the sons of Korah . LORD , thou hast been favorable unto thy land : thou hast brought back the captivity of Jacob.

Psalm 82:1-4
(1)A Psalm of Asaph. God standeth in the congregation of the mighty ; he judgeth among the gods.

(2) How long will ye judge unjustly , and accept the persons of the wicked ? Selah .

(3) Defend the poor and fatherless: do justice to the afflicted and needy .

(4) Deliver the poor and the needy : rid them out of the hand of the wicked.

## February 21

Psalm 82:1
A Psalm of ASAP . God standeth in the congregation of the mighty ; he judgeth among the gods.

Psalm 85:7-9

(7)shew us thy mercy , O LORD , and grant us thy salvation.

(8)I will hear what God the LORD will speak : for he will speak peace unto his people , and to his saints: but let them not turn again to folly.

(9)Surely his salvation is nigh them that fear him ; that glory may dwell in our land.

Psalm 85: 1

To the chief Musician , A Psalm for the sons of Korah . LORD , thou hast been favorable unto thy land : thou hat brought back the captivity of Jacob.

Psalm 85:7

shew us thy mercy , O LORD , and grant us thy salvation

Psalm 85: 10-13

(10)Mercy and truth are met together ; righteousness and peace have kissed each other.

(11)Truth shall spring out of the earth ; and righteousness shall look down from heaven.

(12)Yea, the LORD shall give that which is good ; and our land shall yield her increase .

(13)Righteousness shall go before him; and shall set us in the way of his steps.

Psalm 81: 11

But my people would not hearken to my voice ; and Israel would none of me.

## February 22

Psalm 32:1-2

(1)A Psalm of David , Maschil. Blessed is he whose transgression is forgiven, whose sin is covered.

(2)Blessed is the man unto whom the LORD imputed no iniquity , and in whose spirit there is no guile.

Psalm 35:1

A Psalm of David . Plead my cause , O LORD , with them that

strive with me : fight against them that fight against me.

Psalm 33:1

Rejoice in the LORD . O ye righteous: for praise is comely for the upright.

Psalm 116:14

I will pay my vows unto the LORD now in the presence of all his people.

Psalm 116:13

I will take the cup of salvation , and call upon the name of the LORD.

## February 23

Psalm 68:19

Blessed be the Lord , who daily loadeth us with benefits , even the God of our salvation. Selah.

Esther 5:3-4

(3)Then said the king unto her, What wilt thou , queen Esther ? And what is thy request? It shall be even given thee to the half of the kingdom.

(4)And Esther answered , If it seem good unto the king , let the king and Haman come this day unto the banquet that I have prepared for him.

Psalm 37:10

For yet a little while , and the wicked shall not be: yea , thou shalt diligently consider his place , and it shall not be.

## February 24

Psalm 37:11

But the meek shall inherit the earth ; and shall delight themselves in the abundance of peace.

Psalm 139:16

Thine eyes did see my substance , yet being unperfect ; and in thy book all my members were written , which in continuance were fashioned, when as yet there was none of them.

## February 25

Psalm 48:1

A Song and Psalm for the  sons of Korah . Great is the LORD ,
and greatly to be praised in the city of our God, in the mountain
of his holiness.

Psalm 107:42

The righteous shall see it , and rejoice : and all iniquity shall stop
her mouth.

## February 26

Psalm 82:1

A Psalm of ASAP . God standeth in the congregation of the
mighty;  he judgeth among the gods.

Psalm 85:10

Mercy and truth are met together ; righteousness and peace have
kissed each other.

Psalm 68:29

Because of thy temple at Jerusalem shall kings bring presents
unto thee.

## February 27

Psalm 71:1-2

(1)In thee , O LORD , do I put my trust ; let me never be put to
confusion.

(2)Deliver me in thy righteousness , and cause me to escape :
incline thine ear unto me, and save me.

Psalm 18:6

In my distress I called upon the LORD , and cried unto my God :
he heard my voice out of his temple, and my cry came before
him, even into his ears.

Psalm 19:7
The law of the LORD is perfect , converting the soul: the testimony of the LORD is sure , making wise the simple.

## February 28

Psalm 18:32
It is God that girdeth me with strength , and maketh my way perfect.
Psalm 18: 23-24
(23)I was also upright before him , and I kept myself from mine iniquity.
(24)Therefore hath the LORD recompensed me according to my righteousness, according to the cleanness of my hands in his eyesight.
Psalm 19: 1-3
(1)To the chief Musician , A Psalm of David. The heavens declare the glory of God ; and the firmament sheweth his handiwork.
(2)Day unto day uttered speech , and night sheweth knowledge.
(3)There is no speech nor language, where their voice is not heard.
Psalm 50:10
For every beast of the forest is mine , and the cattle upon a thousand hills.

# March 1

Psalm 27:4

One thing have I desired of the LORD , that will I seek after ; that I may dwell in the house of the LORD all the days of my life , to behold the beauty of the LORD, and to inquire in his temple.

# March 2

Jeremiah 21: 9-12

(9)He that abideth in this city shall die by the sword , and by the famine , and  by the pestilence : but he that goeth out , and falleth to the Chaldeans  that besiege you , he shall live , and his life shall be unto him for a prey.

(10)For I have set my face against this city for evil , and not for good ,saith the LORD : it shall be given into the hand of the king of Babylon, and he shall burn it with fire.

(11)And touching the house of the king of Judah , say, Hear ye the word of the LORD;

(12)O house of David , thus saith the LORD ; Execute judgment in the morning , and deliver him that is spoiled out of the hand of the oppressor , lest my fury go out like fire , and burn that none can quench it , because of the evil of your doings.

Jeremiah 22:3

Thus saith the LORD ; Execute ye judgment and righteousness , and deliver the spoiled out of the hand of the oppressor : and do no wrong , do no violence to the stranger , the fatherless , nor the widow , neither shed innocent blood in this place.

Jeremiah 22:4

For if ye do this thing indeed, then shall there enter in by the gates of this house kings sitting upon the throne of David , riding in chariots and on horses , he , and his servants , and his people.

Psalm 104:27

These wait all upon thee ; that thou mayest give them their meat in due season.

## March 3

Psalm 106:1

Praise ye the LORD . O give thanks unto the LORD ; for he is good: for his mercy endureth for ever.

Psalm 56: 8-13

(8)Thou tallest my wanderings : put thou my tears into thy bottles: are they not in thy book?

(9)When I cry unto thee , then shall mine enemies turn back : this I know ; for God is for me.

(10)In God will I praise his word: in the LORD will I praise his word.

(11)In God have I put my trust : I will not be afraid what man can do unto me.

(12)Thy vows are upon me, O God : I will render praises unto thee.

(13)For thou hast delivered my soul from death : wilt not thou deliver my feet from falling , that I may walk before God in the light of the living?

## March 4

Psalm 57:3

He shall send from heaven , and save me from the reproach of him that would swallow me up. Selah. God shall send forth his mercy and his truth.

Psalm 59:17

Unto thee , O my strength , will I sing : for God is my defence , and the God of my mercy.

Psalm 57:8

Awake up , my glory ; awake, psaltery and harp : I myself will awake early.

Psalm 60:1

To the chief Musician upon Shushaneduth , Michtam of David, to teach ; when he strove with Aramnaharaim and with Aramzobah ,when Joab returned , and smote of Edom in the valley of salt twelve thousand. O God ,thou hast cast us off , thou hast scattered us , thou hast been displeased ; O turn thyself to us again.

Psalm 57: 1

To the chief Musician , Altaschith , Michtam of David , when he fled from Saul in the cave. Be merciful unto me , O GOD ,be merciful unto me:  for my soul trusted in thee : yea , in the shadow of thy wings will I make my refuge, until these calamities be overpast.

Psalm 59:10

The God of my mercy shall prevent me : God shall let me see my desire upon mine enemies.

Psalm 71:1

In thee , O LORD , do I put my trust : let me never be put to confusion.

## March 5

2 Chronicles 25:9

And Amaziah said to the man of God, But what shall we do for the  hundred talents which I have given to the army of Israel ? And the man of God answered , The LORD is able to give thee much more than this.

Deuteronomy 8: 16-18

(16)Who fed thee in the wilderness with manna, which thy fathers knew not , that he might humble thee, and that he might prove thee, to do thee good at thy latter end;

(17)And thou say in thine heart , My power and the might of mine hand hath gotten me this wealth.

(18)But thou shalt remember the LORD thy God : for it is he that giveth thee power to get wealth , that he may

establish his covenant which he sware unto thy fathers , as it is this day.

## March 6

Psalm 116: 13

I will take the cup of salvation , and call upon the name of the LORD.

Psalm 119: 13

With my lips have I declared all the judgments of thy mouth.

Isaiah 60: 16

Thou shalt also suck the milk of the Gentiles , and shalt suck the breast of kings : and thou shalt know that I the LORD am thy Saviour and thy Redeemer , the mighty One of Jacob.

## March 7

Proverbs 15:15

All the days of the afflicted are evil : but he that is of a merry heart hath a continual feast.

Psalm 85: 1

To the chief Musician , A Psalm for the sons of Korah . LORD , thou hast been favorable unto thy land : thou hast brought back the captivity of Jacob.

Psalm 104: 27

These wait all upon thee ; that thou mayest give them their meat in due season.

## March 8

Psalm 106: 4
Remember me , O LORD, with the favour that thou bearest unto thy people : O visit me with thy salvation ;
Psalm 31:14
But I trusted in thee , O LORD : I said , Thou art my God.

## March 9

Psalm 29: 11
The LORD will give strength unto his people ; the LORD will bless his people with peace.
Psalm 28: 7
The LORD is my strength and my shield ; my heart trusted in him , and I am helped :
therefore my heart greatly rejoiceth ; and with my song will I praise him.
Psalm 31:14 -15
(14)But I trusted in thee , O LORD : I said , Thou art my God.
(15)My times are in thy hand : deliver me from the hand of mine enemies , and from them that persecute me.
Psalm 28: 8
The LORD is their strength , and he is the saving strength of his anointed.
1 Kings 2 : 33
Their blood shall therefore return upon the head of Joab ,
and upon the head of his seed for ever : but upon David , and upon his seed, and upon his house , and upon his throne , shall there be peace for ever from the LORD .

## March 10

Psalm 91: 2

I will say of the LORD , He is my refuge and my fortress : my God ; in him will I trust.

Psalm 116:16

O LORD , truly I am thy servant ; I am thy servant , and the son of thine handmaid:  thou hast loosed my bonds.

## March 11

Psalm 82:1

A Psalm of ASAP . God standeth in the congregation of the mighty ; he judgeth among the gods.

Psalm 85: 9

Surely his salvation is nigh them that fear him ; that glory may dwell in our land.

Matthew 6: 33

But seek ye first the kingdom of God , and his righteousness ; and all these things shall be added unto you.

Psalm 116 : 13

I will take the cup of salvation , and call upon the name of the LORD.

## March 12

Psalm 60: 5

That thy beloved may be delivered ; save with thy right hand , and hear me.

Psalm 64: 10

The righteous shall be glad in the LORD , and shall trust in him ; and all the  upright in heart shall glory.

## March 13

Psalm 119:101
I have refrained my feet from every evil way , that I might keep thy word.
Psalm 119: 145
KOPH . I cried with my whole heat ; hear me, O LORD : I will keep thy statutes.
Psalm 60:5
That thy beloved may be delivered ; save with thy right hand, and hear me.

## March 14

Psalm 62: 1
To the chief Musician , to Jeduthun , A Psalm of David .Truly my soul waited upon God : from him cometh my salvation.
Psalm 119: 101
I have refrained my feet from every evil way , that I might keep thy word.
Psalm 119: 105
NUN. Thy word is a lamp unto my feet , and a light unto my path.

## March 15

Psalm 80: 14
Return, we beseech thee , O God of hosts: look down from heaven , and behold , and visit this vine;
Psalm 111:6
He hath shewed his people the power of his works , that he give them the heritage of the heathen.

## March 16

Psalm 116:1
I love the LORD , because he hath heard my voice and my supplications.
Psalm 11:1
To the chief Musician , A Psalm of David. I the LORD put I my trust : how say ye to my soul , Flee as a bird to your mountain.

## March 17

Psalm 9:1-2
(1)To the chief Musician upon Muthlabben , A Psalm of David . I will praise thee , O LORD , with my whole heart ; I will shew forth all thy marvelous works.
(2)I will be glad and rejoice in thee : I will sing praise to thy name, O thou most High .
Psalm 128:2
For thou shalt eat the labour of thine hands : happy shalt thou be, and it shall be well with thee.

## March 18

Psalm 62:1
To the chief Musician , to Jeduthun , A Psalm of David.Truly my soul waited upon God : from him cometh my salvation.
Psalm 80: 17-19
(17)Let thy hand be upon the man of thy right hand , upon the son of man whom thou madest strong for thyself.
(18)So will not we go back from thee: quicken us , and we will call upon thy name.
(19)Turn us again , O LORD God of hosts , cause thy face to shine ; and we shall be saved.

## March 19

Psalm 81:1
To the chief Musician upon Gittith , A Psalm of ASAP . Sing
aloud God our strength : make a joyful noise unto the God of
Jacob.
Psalm 134: 1
A Song of degrees. Behold , bless ye the LORD , all ye
servants of the LORD, which by night stand in the house of the
LORD.

## March 20

Psalm 128:2
For thou shalt eat the labour of thine hands : happy shalt thou be,
and it shall be well with thee.

## March 21

Psalm 135:4
For the LORD hath chosen Jacob unto himself , and Israel for his
peculiar treasure.
Psalm 59:10
The God of me mercy shall prevent me: God shall let me see my
desire upon mine enemies.

## March 22

Psalm 57: 5-8
(5)Be thou exalted , O God , above the heavens ; let thy glory be
above all the earth.
(6)They have prepared a net for my steps ; my soul is bowed
down : they have digged a pit before me, into the midst whereof

they are fallen themselves , Selah.

(7)My heart id fixed , O God , my heart is fixed : I will sing and give praise.

(8)Awake up , my glory ; awake , psaltery and harp : I myself will awake early.

Psalm 7: 9-10

(9)Oh let the wickedness of the wicked come to and end ; but establish the just : for the righteous God trieth the hearts and reins .

(10)My defence is of God , which saveth the upright in heart.

## March 23

Psalm 19: 1-7

(1)To the Musician , A Psalm of David. The heavens declare the glory of God ; and the firmament sheweth his handiwork.

(2)Day unto day uttered speech , and night sheweth knowledge.

(3)There is no speech nor language, where their voice is not heard.

(4)Their line is gone out through all the earth , and their words to the end of the world. In them hath he set a tabernacle  for the sun,

(5)Which is a bridegroom coming out of his chamber , and rejoiceth as a strong man to run a race.

(6)His going forth is from the end of the heaven , and his circuit undto the ends of it : and there is nothing hid from the heat thereof.

(7)The law of the LORD is perfect , converting the soul : the testimony of the LORD is sure , making wise the simple.

Psalm 96: 10-13

(10)Say among the heathen that the LORD reigneth : the world also shall be established that it shall not be moved ; he shall judge the people righteously.

(11)Let the heavens rejoice , and let the earth be  glad ; let the sea roar , and the fulness thereof.

(12)Let the field be joyful , and all that is therein : then shall all the trees of the wood rejoice

(13)Before the LORD ; for he cometh , for he cometh to judge earth : he shall judge the world with righteousness , and the people with his truth.

Psalm 102:1

A Prayer of the afflicted , when he is overwhelmed , and poureth out his complaint before the LORD. Hear my prayer , O LORD , and let my cry come unto thee.

## March  24

Psalm 102: 1

A prayer of the afflicted , when he is overwhelmed , and poureth out his complaint before the LORD . Hear my prayer , O LORD , and let my cry come unto thee.

Psalm 96:12

Let the field be joyful , and all that is therein : then shall all the trees of the wood rejoice

Psalm 97: 1

The LORD reigneth ; let the earth rejoice ; let the multitude of isles be glad thereof.

Psalm 99: 6

Honour and majesty are before him: strength and beauty are in his sanctuary.

Psalm 116:13-19

(13)I will take the cup of salvation , and call upon the name of the LORD.

(14)I will pay my vows unto the LORD now in the presence of all his people.

(15)Precious in the sight of the LORD is the death of his saints.

(16)O LORD , truly I am thy servant ; I am thy servant , and the son of thine handmaid : thou hast loosed my bonds.

(17)I will offer to thee the sacrifice of thanksgiving , and will call upon the name of the LORD.

(18)I will pay my vows unto the LORD now in the presence of all his people,

(19)In the courts of the Lord's house , in the midst of thee , O Jerusalem . Praise ye the LORD.

## March 25

Psalm 119:24

Thy testimonies also are my delight and my counselors.

Genesis 48:16

The Angel which redeemed me from all evil , bless the lads ; and let my name be named on them , and the name of my fathers Abraham and Isaac ; and let them grow into a multitude in the midst of the earth.

Psalm 40: 12-13

(12)For innumerable evils have compassed me about : mine iniquities have taken hold upon me, so that I am not able to look up ; they are more than the hairs of mine head : therefore my heart faileth me.

(13)Be pleased , O LORD , to deliver me: O LORD , make haste to help me.

## March 26

Psalm 37:28

For the LORD loveth judgmemt , and forsaketh not his saints ; they are preserved for ever: but the seed of the wicked shall be cut off.

Psalm 40: 1

To the chief Musician , A Psalm of David . I waited patiently for the Lord ; and he inclined unto me, and herd my cry.

Psalm 111:7

The works of his hands are verity and judgmemt ; all his commandments are sure.

Psalm 40:13

Be pleased , O LORD , to deliver me: O LORD , make haste to help me.

## March 27

Psalm 44:1

To the Chief Musician for the sons of Korah , Mashil. We have heard with our ears , O God ,our fathers have told us , what work thou didst in their days , in the times of old.

Psalm 40:13

Be pleased , O LORD , to deliver me : O LORD , make haste to help me.

Psalm 31:14

But I trusted in thee , O LORD : I said , Thou art my God

Psalm 28: 4

Give them according to their deeds , and according to the wickedness of their endeavours : give them after the work of their hands ; render to them their desert.

Psalm 28:7

The LORD is my strength and my shield ; my heart trusted in him , and I am helped : therefore my heat greatly rejoiceth ; and with my song will I praise him.

## March 28

1 Chronicles 22:19
Now set your heart and your soul to seek the LORD your God ;
arise therefore , and build ye the sanctuary of the LORD God, to
bring the ark of the covenant of the LORD , and the holy vessels
of God , into the house that is to be built to the name o the
LORD.
Psalm 56:11
In God have I put my trust : I will not be afraid what man
can do unto me.
Psalm 56: 8 - 9
(8)Thou tellest my wanderings : put thou my tears into thy
bottle: are they not in thy book?
(9)When I cry unto thee, then shall mine
enemies turn back : this I know ; for God is for me.

## March 29

Psalm 59:17
Unto thee , O my strength , will I sing: for God is my defence ,
and the God of my mercy.
Psalm 81:11
But my people would not hearken to my voice ; and Israel would
none of me.
Psalm 85:1
To the chief Musician , A Psalm for the sons of Korah . LORD ,
thou hast been favorable unto thy land: thou hast
brought back the captivity of Jacob.

## March 30

Psalm 84:11

For the LORD God is a sun and shield: the LORD will give grace and glory : no good thing will he withhold from them that walk uprightly.

Psalm 104:1

Bless the LORD, O my soul. O LORD my God, thou art very great; thou art clothed with honour and majesty.

## March 31

Psalm 103:1

A Psalm of David . Bless the LORD , o my soul: and all that is within me , bless his holy name.

Psalm 102:12

But thou , O LORD, shalt endure for ever ; and thy remembrance unto all generations.

Psalm 104:1

Bless the LORD, O my soul. O LORD my God , thiu art very great ; thou art clothed with honour and majesty.

Psalm 116:14

O LORD , truly I am thy servant ; I am thy servant , and the son of thine handmaid: thou hat loosed my bonds.

## April 1

Psalm 105 : 1
O give thanks unto the Lord ; call upon his name: make known
his deeds among the people.
Psalm 19 : 7
The law of the LORD is perfect , converting the soul :
the testimony of the LORD is sure , making wise the simple.

## April 2

Psalm 135 : 1
Praise ye the Lord . Praise ye the name of the Lord; praise him ,
O ye servants of the Lord.
Psalm 85:1
To the chief Musician , A Psalm for the sons of Korah . LORD ,
thou hast been favourable unto thy land: thou hast brought back
the captivity of Jacob.

## April 3

Psalm 106 : 5
That I may see the good of thy chosen , that I may rejoice in the
gladness of thy nation , that I may glory with thine inheritance.
Psalm 68 : 19
Blessed the Lord , who daily loadeth us with benifits , even the
God of our salvation . Selah.

## April 4

Isaiah 66: 5
Hear the word of the LORD, ye that tremble at his word ; Your

brethen that hated you , that cast you out for my name's sake , said , Let the LORD be glorified : but he shall appear to your joy , and they shall be ashamed.

Isaiah 66 : 16

For by fire and by his sword will the LORD plead with all flesh : and the slain of the LORD shall be many.

Job 13 : 15

Though he slay me , yet will I trust in him: but I will maintain mine own ways before him.

Psalm 66:1

To the chief Musician , A Song or Psalm .Make a joyful noise unto God all ye lands:

Psalm 68:11

The Lord gave the word: great was the company of those that published it.

## April 5

Psalm 65:10

Thou waterest the ridges thereof abundantly : thou settlest the furrows thereof : thou makest it soft with showers: thou blessest the springing thereof.

Psalm 67: 1

To the chief Musician on Neginoth , A Psalm or Song. God be merciful unto us , and bless us  and cause his face to shine upon us; Selah.

Better is a dinner of herbs where love is , than a stalled ox and hatred therewith.

Psalm 65:1

To the chief Musician , A Palm and Song of David. Praise waited for thee , O God , in Sion : and unto thee shall the vow be preformed.

Proverbs 15 :16
Better is little with the fear of the LORD than great treasure and trouble therewith.

## April 6

Psalm 104 :28
That thou givest them they gather : thou openest thine hand , they are filled with good.
Psalm 12: 5
For the oppression of the poor , for the sighing of the needy, now will I arise , saith the LORD ; I will set him in safety from him that puffeth at him.

## April 7

Psalm 80:18-19
(18)So will not we go back from thee : quicken us , and we will call upon thy name.
(19)Turn us again , O LORD God of hosts , caus thy face to shine ; and we shall be saved.
Psalm 80:17
Let thy hand be upon the man of thy right hand , upon the son of man whom thou madest strong for thyself.
Psalm 71 :8
Let my mouth be filled with thy praise and with thy honour all the day.

## April 8

Psalm 119: 145
KOPH. I cried with my whole heart ; hear me , O LORD : I will keep thy statues.
Psalm 119 : 101
I have refrained my feet from every evil way, that I might keep

thy word.

Psalm 119 : 105

NUN. Thy word is a lamp unto my feet , and a light unto my path.

Psalm 116:13

I will take the cup of salvation , and call upon the name of the LORD.

## April 9

Psalm 82:1

A Psalm of ASAP . God standeth in the congregation of the mighty ; he judgeth among the gods.

Psalm 85:9

Surely his salvation is nigh them that fear him; that glory may dwell in our land.

Psalm 119:10

With my whole heart have I sought thee : O let me not wander from thy commandments.

Psalm 119 :157

Many are my persecutors and mine enemies ; yet do I not decline from thy testimonies.

Psalm 119: 105

NUN. Thy word is a lamp unto my feet , and a light unto my path.

## April 10

Psalm 104 :28

That thou givest them they gather : thou openest thine hand , they are filled with good.

Psalm 104: 27

These wait all upon thee : that thou mayest give them their meat in due season.

Psalm 59: 10
The God of my mercy shall prevent me : God shall let me see my desire upon mine enemies.

## April 11

Psalm 40:1
I waited patiently for the Lord : and he inclined unto me , and head my cry.
Psalm 40 :13
Be pleased , O LORD , to deliver me: O LORD , make haste to help me.
2 Thessalonians 5:24
Faithful is he that calleth you , who also will do it .
Philippians 1 : 6
Being confident of this very thing , that he which hath begun a good work in you will perform it until the day of Jesus Christ.
Psalm 106:3
Blessed are they that keep judgement , and he that doeth righteousness at all times.

## April 12

Psalm 4: 1
HEAR me when I call , O God of my righteousness : thou hast enlarged me when I was in distress ; have mercy upon me, and hear my prayer.
Psalm 135: 4-6
(4)For the Lord hath chosen Jacob unto himself , and Isreal for his peculiar treasure.
(5)For I know that the Lord is great , and that our Lord is above all gods.
(6)Whatsoever the Lord pleased , that did he in heaven , and in

earth , in the seas , and all deep places.
Proverbs 15:16
Better  is little with the fear of the LORD than great treasure and trouble therewith.

## April 13

Psalm 89:24
But my faithfulness and my mercy shall be with him : and in my name shall his horn be exalted.

## April 14

Psalm 117:1-2
(1)O Praise the LORD , all ye nations : praise him , all ye people. (2)For his merciful kindness is great toward us : and the truth of the LORD endureth for ever. Praise ye the LORD.
Matthew 10:16
Behold , I send you forth as shee in themidst of wolves : be ye therefore wise as serpents , and harmless as doves.
Psalm 143 : 6
I stretch forth my hands unto thee : my soul thirsteth after thee , as a thirsty land. Selah .
Psalm 70:1
To the chief Musician , A Psalm of David , to bring to remembrance. Make haste , O God , to deliver me ; make

## April 15

Psalm 68: 29
Because of thy temple at Jerusalem shall kings bring presents unto thee.
Psalm 17:15
As for me , I will behold thy face in righteousness : I shall be

satisfied , when I awake , with thy likeness.

## April 16

Psalm 70:1
To the chief Musician , A Psalm of David , to bring to
remembrance . Make haste , O God , to deliver me ; make haste
to help me , O LORD.
Psalm 71:1
In thee , O LORD , do I put my trust : let me never be put to
confusion .
Psalm 69:36
The seed also of his servants shall inherit it : and they that love
his name shall dwell therein.
Psalm 51:19
Then shalt thou be pleased with the sacrifices of righteousness ,
with  burnt offering and whole burnt offering : then shall they
offer bullocks upon thine altar.
Psalm 55:1
To the chief Musician on Neginoth , Maschil , A Psalm of David .
Give ear to my prayer , O God ; and hide not thyself from my
supplication.

## April 17

Psalm 56:1
To the chief Musician upon Jonathelemrechokim , Michtam of
David , when  the Philistines took him in
Gath . Be merciful unto me , O God : for man would swallow me
up ; he fighting daily oppresseth me .
Psalm 59:17
Unto thee , O my strength , will I sing : for God is my defence ,
and the God of my mercy.
Isaiah 6: 7-8
(7)And he laid it upon my mouth , and said , Lo , this hath

touched thy lips ; and thine iniquity is taken away , and thy sin purged.

(8)Also I heard the voice of the Lord , saying , Whom shall I send , and who will go for us ? Then said I , Here am I ; send me.

Psalm 31:14

But I rusted in thee , O LORD : I said , Thou art my God.

## April 18

Psalm 29:11

The Lord will give strength unto his people ; the LORD will bless his people with peace.

## April 19

Psalm 34:18

The Lord is nigh unto them that are a broken heart ; and saveth such as be of a contrite spirit.

Psalms 145 : 7

They shall abundantly utter the memory of thy great goodness , and shall sing of thy righteousness.

Psalm 147: 10-11

(10)He delighted not in the strength of the horse : he taketh not pleasure in the legs of a man.

(11)The LORD taketh pleasure in them that fear him , in those that hope in his mercy.

## April 20

Psalm 144: 5 -7

(5)Bow thy heavens , O LORD , and come down : touch the mountains , and they shall smoke.

(6)Cast forth lightning , and scatter them : shoot out thine arrows

, and destroy them.

(7)Send thine hand from above ; rid me , and deliver me out of great waters, from the hand of strange children;

Psalm 107:1

O give thanks unto the LORD , for he is good : for his mercy endureth for ever.

Psalm 37: 28-29

(28)For the LORD loveth judgment , and forsaketh not his saints ; the are preserved for ever : but the seed of the wicked shall be cut off.

(29)The righteous shall inherit the land , and dwell therein for ever .

## April 21

Psalm 35 : 1-3

(1)A Psalm of David . Plead my cause , O LORD , with them that strive with me : fight against them that fight against me .

(2)Take hold of shield and buckler , and stand up for mine help .

(3)Draw out also the spear , and stop the way against them that persecute me : say unto my soul , I am thy salvation.

Psalms 35:2

Take hold of shield and buckler , and stand up for mine help.

Psalm 128 : 4-6

(4)Behold , that thus shall the man be blessed that feareth the LORD.

(5)The LORD shall bless thee out of Zion : and thou shalt see the good of Jerusalem all the days of thy life.

(6)Yea , thou shalt see thy children's children , and peace upon Israel.

## April 22

Psalm 128 : 1

A Song of degrees . Blessed is every one that feareth the LORD ;

that walketh in his ways.

Psalm 116 : 10

I believed , therefore have I spoken : I was greatly afflicted:

Psalm 119 : 17

GIMEL. Deal bountifully with thy servant , that I may live , and keep thy word.

Psalm 119 : 16

I will delight myself in thy statutes : I will not forget thy word.

## April 23

Psalm 102 : 1

A Prayer of the afflicted , when he is overwhelmed and poureth out his complaint before the LORD . Hear my prayer , O LORD , let my cry come unto thee.

Jeremiah 31 : 4

Again I will build thee , and thou shalt be built , O virgin of Israel : thou shalt again be adorned with thy tabrets , and shalt go forth in the dances of them that make merry.

## April 24

Job 2 : 2

And the LORD said unto Satan , From whence comest thou ? And Santan answered the LORD , and said , From going to and fro in the earth , and from walking up and down in it.

Psalm 31 : 14

But I trust in thee, O LORD : I said , Thou art my God.

Psalm 119 : 105

NUN . Thy word is a lamp unto my feet, and a light unto my path.

# April 25

Psalm 119 : 165
Great peace have they which love thy law : and nothing shall offend them.
Psalm 119 : 52
I remembered thy judgments of old , O LORD ; and have comforted myself.

# April 26

Psalm 3 : 6
I will not be afraid of ten thousands of people , that have set themselves against me round about.
Psalm 5 : 1
To the chief  Musician upon Nehiloth , A Psalm of David . Give ear to my words , O LORD , consider my meditation .
Psalm 146 : 8
The LORD openeth the eyes of the blind : the LORD raiseth them that are bowed down : the LORD loveth the righteous :
Psalm 40 : 1
To the chief Musician , A Psalm of David . I waited patiently for the LORD ; and he inclined unto me , and heard my cry.

# April 27

Psalm 11: 1
To the chief Musician , A Psalm of David . In the LORD put I my trust: how say ye to my soul , Flee as a bird to your mountain?
Psalm 12 : 1
To the chief Musician upon Sheminith , A Psalm of David . Help , LORD ; for the godly man ceaseth ; for the faithful fail from among the children of men.

Psalm 11 : 7

For the righteous LORD loveth righteousness ; his countenance doth behold the upright .

Psalm 11 : 4

The LORD is in his holy temple , the LORD'S throne is in heaven : his eyes behold , his eyelids try , the children of men.

Psalm 106 : 1

Praise ye the LORD . O give thanks unto the LORD ; for he is good : for his mercy endureth for ever.

## April 28

Psalm 104 : 24

O LORD , how manifold are thy works ! In wisdom hast thou made them all : the earth is full of thy riches.

Psalm 92 : 8

But thou , LORD , art most high for evermore.

## April 29

Psalm 96 : 1

O sing unto the LORD a new song : sing unto the LORD , all the earth.

Psalm 92 : 4

For thou , LORD , hast made me glad through thy work: I will triumph in the works of thy hands.

Jeremiah 31 : 16 - 17

(16)Thus saith the LORD ; Refrain thy voice from weeping , and thine eyes from tears : for thy work shall be rewarded , saith the LORD ; and they shall come again from the land of the enemy. (17)And there is hope in thine end , saith the LORD , that thy children shall come again to their own border .

# April 30

Psalm 68 : 19
Blessed be the Lord , who daily loadeth us with benefits , even
the God of our salvation . Selah .
Psalm 92 : 4
For thou , LORD , hast made me glad through thy work : I will
triumph in the works of thy hands.

## May 1

Psalm 94 : 1 -2

(1)O LORD God , to whom vengeance belongeth , shew thyself. (2)Lift up thyself , thou judge of the earth : render a reward to the proud.

Psalm 96 : 1

O sing unto the LORD a new song : sing unto the LORD , all the earth.

Psalm 95 : 7

For he is our God ; and we are the people of his pasture , and the sheep of his hand . To day if ye will hear his voice.

## May 2

Psalm 19 : 6 - 7

(6)His going forth is from the end of the heaven , his circuit unto the ends of it : and there is nothing hi from the heat thereof. (7)The law of the LORD is perfect , converting the soul : the testimony of the LORD is sure , making wise the simple .

Psalm 78 : 39

For he remembered that they were but flesh ; a wind that passeth away , and cometh not again .

Psalm 79 : 12

And render unto our neighbors sevenfold into their bosom their reproach , wherewith they have reproached thee, O Lord .

## May 3

Psalm 78: 1

Maschil of ASAP . Give ear , O my people , to my law : incline your ears to the words of my mouth.

Psalm 77 : 20

Thou leddest thy people like a flock by the hand of Moses and Aaron .

Psalm 40 : 13
Be pleased , O LORD , to deliver me : O LORD , make haste to help me.

## May 4

Psalm 71 : 13 -14
(13)Let them be confounded and consumed that are adversaries to my soul ; let them be covered with reproach and dishonour that seek my hurt .
(14)But I will hope continually , and will yet praise thee more and more.
Psalm 28 : 7
The LORD is my strength and my shield ; my heart trusted in him , and I am helped : therefore my heart greatly rejoiceth ; and with my song will I praise him.

## May 5

Psalm 31 : 14
But I trusted in thee , O LORD : I said , Thou art my God.
Psalm 104 : 27
These wait all upon thee ; that thou mayest give them their meat in due season.

## May 6

Psalm 106 : 4
Remember me , O LORD , with the favour that thou bearest unto thy people: O visit me with thy salvation;
Psalm 12 : 7
Thou shalt keep them , O LORD , thou shalt preserve them from this generation for ever.

## May 7

Ezekiel 36 : 26 – 27

(26)A new heart also will I give you , and a new spirit will I put within you: and I will take away the stony heart out of your flesh , and I will give you an heart of flesh.

(27)And I will put my spirit within you , and cause you to walk in my statutes , and ye shall keep my judgments , and do them.

Psalm 105 : 45

That they might observe his statutes , and keep his laws. Praise ye the LORD.

## May 8

Psalm 139 : 23

Search me , O God , and know my heart : try me , and know my thoughts:

Psalm 140 : 11

Let not an evil speaker be established in the earth : evil shall hunt the violent man to overthrow him.

Psalm 143 : 10

Teach me to do thy will ; for thou art my God : thy spirit is good ; lead me into the land of uprightness.

Psalm 59 : 14 - 17

(14)And at evening let them return ; let them make a noise like a dog , and go round about the city.

(15)Let them wander up and down for meat , and grudge if they be not satisfied.

(16)But I will sing of thy power ; yea, I will sing aloud of thy mercy in the morning : for thou hast been my defence and refuge in the day of my trouble.

(17)Unto thee , O my strength , will I sing : for God is my defence , and the God of my mercy.

## May 9

Isaiah 59 : 2

But your iniquities have separated between you and your God ,
and your sins have hid his face from you , that he will not hear.

Psalm 143 : 4 - 6

(4)Therefore is my spirit overwhelmed within me ; my heart
within me is desolate.

(5)I remember the days of old ; I meditate on all thy works ; I
muse in the work of thy hands.

(6)I stretch forth my hands unto thee : my soul thirsteth after
thee , as a thirsty land . Selah .

Jeremiah 50 : 18 - 20

(18)Therefore thus saith the LORD of hosts, the God of Israel ;
behold , I will punish the king of Babylon and his land , as I have
punished the king of Assyria.

(19)And I will bring Israel again to his habitation , and he shall
feed on Carmel and Bashan , and his soul shall be satisfied upon
mount Ephraim and Gilead.

(20)In those days , and in that time , saith the LORD , the iniquity
of Israel shall be sought for , and there shall be none ; and the
sins of Judah , and they shall not be found : for I will pardon
them whom I reserve.

Psalm 40 : 13

Be pleased , O LORD , to deliver me : O LORD , make haste to
help me .

## May 10

Psalm 107 : 42

The righteous shall see it , and rejoice : and all iniquity shall stop
her mouth.

Psalm 57 : 8 - 11

(8)Awake up , my glory ; awake , psaltery and harp : I myself will awake early .

(9)I will praise thee , O Lord , among the people : I will sing unto thee among the nations.

(10)For thy mercy is great unto the heavens , and thy truth unto the clouds .

(11)Be thou exalted , O God , above the heavens : let thy glory be above all the earth.

Psalm 57 : 5

Be thou exalted , O God , above the heavens ; let thy glory be above all the earth.

## May 11

Isaiah 29 : 23

But when he seeth his children , the work of mine hands , in the midst of him , they shall sanctify my name , and sanctify the Holy One of Jacob , and shall fear the God of Israel.

Psalm 148 : 7

Praise the LORD from the earth , ye dragons , and all deeps :

Psalm 119 : 105

NUN . Thy word is a lamp unto my feet , and a light unto my path.

## May 12

Psalm 119 : 159 - 160

(159)Consider how I love thy precepts: quicken me , O LORD , according to thy lovingkindness.

(160)Thy word is true from the beginning : and every one of thy righteous judgments endureth for ever .

Psalm 111: 1

Praise ye the LORD . I will praise the LORD with my whole heart

, in the assembly of the upright , and in the congregation .
Psalm 116 : 1
I love the LORD , because he hath heard my voice and my supplications.

**May 13**


Psalm 115 : 15
Ye are blessed of the LORD which made heaven and
earth.
Psalm 56 : 4
In God I will praise his word , in God I have put my trust ; I will not fear what flesh can do unto me.
Psalm 57 : 5
Be thou exalted , O God , above the heavens ; let thy glory be above all the earth.

**May 14**


Psalm 59 : 13
Consume them in wrath , consume them , that they may not be : and let them know that God ruleth in Jacob unto the ends of the earth.
Psalm 56 : 13
For thou hast delivered my soul from death : wilt not
thou deliver my feet from falling , that I may walk before God in the light of the living?

**May 15**


Psalm 3 : 6
I will not be afraid of ten thousands of people , that have set themselves against me round about.
Psalm 2 : 8
Ask of me , and I shall give thee the heathen for thine inheritance , and the uttermost parts of the earth for thy possession .

Psalm 4 : 1

To the chief Musician on Neginoth , A Psalm of David . Hear me when I call , O God of my righteousness : thou hast enlarged me when I was in distress ; have mercy upon me , and hear my prayer.

## May 16

Psalm 7 : 12

If he turn not , he will whet his sword ; he hath bent his bow , and made it ready.

Psalm 5 : 1

To the chief Musician upon Nehiloth , A Psalm of David .Give ear to my words , O LORD , consider my meditation .

## May 17

Psalm 57 : 8 - 9

(8)Awake up , my glory ; awake , psaltery and harp : I myself will awake early.

(9)I will praise thee , O Lord , among the people : I will sing unto thee among the nations.

Psalm 121 : 1 -2

(1)A Song of degrees . I will lift up mine eyes unto the hills , from whence cometh my help.

(2)My help cometh from the LORD , which made heaven and earth.

## May 18

Psalm 127 : 1

A Song of degrees for Solomon . Except the LORD build the house , they labour in vain that build it : except the LORD keep the city , the watchman walketh but in vain.

Psalm 7 : 9

Oh let the wickedness of the wicked come to an end ; but establish the just : for the righteous God trieth the hearts and reins.

Psalm 81 : 13

So I gave them up unto their own hearts lust : and they walked in their own counsels.

Psalm 85 : 12

Yea , the LORD shall give that which is good ; and our land shall yield her increase.

Psalm 85 : 1

To the chief Musician , A Psalm for the sons of Korah . LORD , thou hast been favorable unto thy land : thou hast brought back the captivity of Jacob.

**May 19**

Psalm 83 : 1

A Song or Psalm of Asaph. Keep not thou silence , O God : hold not thy peace , and be not still , O God.

Psalm 116 : 1

I love the LORD , because he hath heard my voice and my supplications.

**May 20**

Psalm 116 : 2

Because he hath inclined his ear unto me , therefore will I call upon him as long as I live.

Psalm 65 : 7

Which stilleth the noise of the seas , the noise of their waves , and the tumult of the people.

Psalm 65 : 10

Thou waterest the ridges thereof abundantly : thou settlest the furrows thereof : thou blesses the springing thereof .

## May 21

Psalm 113 : 1
Praise ye the LORD . Praise , O ye servants of the LORD , praise the name of the LORD.
Psalm 116 : 1
I love the LORD , because he hath heard my voice and me supplications.

## May 22

Psalm 139 : 23 - 24
(23)Search me , O God , and know my heart : try me , and know my thoughts:
(24)And see if there be any wicked way in me , and lead me in the way everlasting .
Psalm 12 : 7
Thou shalt keep them , O Lord , thou shalt preserve them from this generation for ever.
Psalm 12 : 5 -7
(5)For the oppression of the poor , for the sighing of the needy now , ;will I arise ,
saith the Lord ; I will set him in safety from him that puffeth at him.
(6)The words of the Lord re pure words : as silver tried in a furnace of earth , purified seven times.
(7)Thou shalt keep them , O Lord , thou shalt preserve them from this generation for ever.

## May 23

Psalm 59 : 17
Unto thee , O my strength , will I sing : for God is my defence , and the God of my mercy.

Psalm 59 : 16

But I will sing of thy power : yea , I will sing aloud of thy mercy in the morning : for thou hast been my defence and refuge in the day of my trouble.

Psalm 59 : 13

Consume them in wrath , consume them , that they may not be : and let them know that God ruleth in Jacob unto the ends of the earth . Selah.

Psalm 56 : 9

When I cry unto thee , then shall mine enemies turn back : this I know ; for God is for me.

## May 24

Psalm 32 : 1

BLESSED is he whose transgression is forgiven , whose sin is covered .

Psalm 34 : 14

Depart from evil , and do good ; seek peace , and pursue it.

Psalm 34 : 13

Keep thy tongue from evil , and thy lips from speaking guile.

Psalm 35 : 1

PLEAD my cause , O Lord with them that strive with me : fight against them that fight against me.

## May 25

Psalm 28 : 7

The Lord is my strength and my shield : my heart trusted in him , and I am helped : therefore my heart greatly rejoiceth ; and with my song will I praise him.

Psalm 12 : 7 -8

(7)Thou shalt keep them , O Lord , thou shalt preserve them from this generation for ever.

(8)The wicked walk on every side , when the vilest men are exalted .

## May 26

Psalm 17 : 15

As for me , I will behold thy face in righteousness : I shall be satisfied , when I awake , with thy likeness.

Psalm 128: 2

For thou shalt eat the labour of thine hands : happy shalt thou be , and it shall be well with thee.

## May 27

Psalm 135 : 4

For the LORD hath chosen Jacob unto himself , and Israel for his peculiar treasure.

Psalm 128 : 2

For thou shalt eat the labour of thine hands : happy shalt thou be , and it shall be well with thee.

## May 28

Psalm 139 : 23

Search me , O God , and know my heart : try me , and know my thoughts:

Psalm 143 : 10

Teach me to do thy will ; for thou art my God : thy spirit is good ; lead me into the land of uprightness.

Isaiah 11: 2

And the spirit of the Lord shall rest upon him , the spirit of wisdom and understanding , the spirit of counsel and might , the spirit of knowledge and of the fear of the Lord:

## May 29

Joel 2 : 32
And it shall come to pass , that whosoever shall call on the name
of the Lord shall be delivered : for in mount Zion and in
Jerusalem  shall be deliverance , as the Lord hath said , and in the
remnant whom the Lord shall call .
Psalm 134 : 1- 3
(1)A Song of degrees . Behold , bless ye the LORD , all
ye servants of the LORD , all which by night stand in the
house of the LOD.
(2)Lift up your hands in the sanctuary , and bless the LORD .
(3)The LORD that made heaven and earth bless thee out of Zion.

## May 30

Psalm 128 : 2
For thou shalt eat the labour of thine hands: happy shalt thou be ,


and it shall be well with thee.
Isaiah 43 : 18 - 19
(18)Remember ye not the former things , neither consider the
things of old.
(19)Behold , I will do a new thing ; now it shall spring forth ;
shall ye not know it?
## May 31

Isaiah 43 : 18 -19
(18)Remember ye not the former things , neither
consider the things of old .

(19)Behold , I will do a new thing ; now it shall spring forth ; shall ye not know it ?

Isaiah 44 : 1 -2

(1)Yet now hear , O Jacob my servant ; and Israel , whom I have chosen :

(2)Thus saith the LORD that made the , and formed thee from the womb , which will help thee ; Fear not , O Jacob , my servant ; and thou , Jesurun , whom I have chosen .

## June 1

Isaiah 44 : 3
For I will pour water upon him that is thirsty , and floods upon
the dry ground : I will pour my spirit upon thy seed
, and my blessing upon thy seed , and my blessing  upon thine
offspring :
Isaiah 44 : 26
Thus saith the LORD the King of Israel , and his redeemer  the
LORD of hosts ; I am the first , and I am the last ; and beside me
there is no  God .
Isaiah 43 : 18 - 19
(18)Remember ye not the former things , neither consider the
things of old .
(19)Behold , I will do a new thing ; now it shall spring forth ;
shall ye not know it ? I will even make a way in the wilderness ,
and rivers in the desert .

## June 2

Deuteronomy 31 : 7
And Moses called unto Joshua , and said unto him in the sight of
all Israel , Be strong and of a good courage : for thou must go
with this people unto the land which the
LORD hath sworn unto their fathers to give them ; and thou
shalt cause them to inherit it .
Joshua 1: 6
Be strong and of a good courage : for unto this people shalt thou
divide for am inheritance the land , which I sware unto their
fathers to give them.
Psalm 11: 1
To the chief musician , A Psalm of David . In the LORD put I my
trust : how say ye to my soul , Flee as a bird to your mountain?

Isaiah 60 : 16

Thou shalt also suck the milk of the Gentiles , and shalt suck the breast of kings : and thou shalt know that I th LORD am thy Saviour and the Redeemer , the mighty One of Jacob.

Isaiah 60 : 1

Arise , shine ; for thy light is come , and the glory of the LORD is risen upon thee.

## June 3

Psalm 139 : 23

Search me , O God , and know my heart : try me , and know my thoughts:

Psalm 139 : 12 - 13

(12)Yea , the darkness hideth not from thee ; but the night shineth as the day : the darkness and the light are both alike to thee.

(13)For thou hast possessed my reins : thou hast covered me in my mother's womb .

Psalm 140 : 1

To the chief Musician , A Psalm of David . Deliver me , O LORD , from the evil man : preserve me from the violent man;

## June 4

Psalm 143 : 8

Cause me to hear thy lovingkindness in the morning ; for in thee do I trust : cause me to know the way wherein I should walk ; for I lift up my soul unto thee.

Psalm 128 : 2

For thou shalt eat the labour of thine hands : happy shalt thou be , and it shall be well with thee.

## June 5

Psalm 135 : 4
For the LORD hath chosen Jacob unto himself , and Israel for his peculiar treasure .
Psalm 135 : 3
Praise the LORD ; for the LORD is good : sing praises
unto his name; for it is pleasant.

## June 6

Proverbs 7: 1
My son , keep my words , and lay up my commandments with thee.
Psalm 135 : 5
For I know that the LORD is great , and that our Lord is above all gods .

## June 7

Psalm 131 : 1 - 3
(1)A Song of degrees of David . LORD , my heart is not haughty , nor mine eyes lofty : neither do I exercise myself in great matters , or in things too high for me .
(2)Surely I have behaved and quieted myself , as a child that is weaned of his mother : my soul is even as a weaned child.
 (3)Let Israel hope in the LORD from henceforth and for ever.
Psalm 56 : 8 - 11
(8)Thou tallest my wanderings : put thou my tears into thy bottle : are they not in thy book?
(9)When I cry unto thee , then shall mine enemies turn back : this I know ; for God is for me.
(10)In God will I praise his word : in the LORD will I praise his word.

(11)In God have I put my trust : I will not be afraid what man can do unto me .

## June 8

Psalm 56 : 13

For thou hast delivered my soul from death : wilt not thou deliver my feet from falling , that I may walk before God in the light of the living.

Psalm 134 : 1

A Song of degrees .Behold , bless ye the LORD , all ye servants of the LORD , which by night stand in the house of the LORD.

## June 9

Psalm 131 : 1 -3

(1)A Song of degrees of David . LORD , my heart is not haughty , nor mine eyes lofty : neither do I exercise myself in great matters , or in things too high for me .

(2)Surely I have behaved and quieted myself , as a child that is weaned of his mother : my soul is even a weaned child .

(3)Let Israel hope in the LORD from henceforth and for ever .

Psalm 128 : 2

For thou shalt eat the labour of thine hands : happy shalt thou be , and it shall be well with thee.

## June 10

Psalm 135 : 1

Praise ye the LORD . Praise ye the name of the LORD ; praise him , O ye servants of the LORD .

Psalm 59 : 13

Consume them in wrath , consume them , that they may not be : and let them know that God ruleth in Jacob unto

the ends of the earth . Selah .
Psalm 59 : 16
But I will sing of thy power ; yea , I will sing aloud of thy mercy
in the morning : for thou hast been my defence
and refuge in the day of my trouble.

## June 11

Psalm 59 : 16
But I will sing of thy power ; yea , I will sing aloud of thy mercy
in the morning : for thou hast been my defence and refuge in the
day of my trouble.
Isaiah 48 : 20
Go ye forth of Babylon , flee ye from the Chaldeans , with a voice
of singing declare ye , tell this, utter it even to the of the earth ;
say ye , The LORD hath redeemed his servant Jacob.

## June 12

Isaiah 48 : 17
Thus saith the LORD , thy Redeemer , the Holy One of Israel ; I
am the LORD thy God which teacheth thee to profit , which
leadeth thee by the way that thou shouldest go.
Psalm 57 : 8
Awake up , my glory ; awake , psaltery and harp : I myself will
awake early .
Psalm 59 : 12
For the sin of their mouth and the words of their lips let them
even be taken in their pride : and for cursing and lying which
they speak.
Psalm 59 : 17
Unto thee , O my strength , will I sing : for God is my defence ,
and the God of my mercy.

Psalm 57 : 11

Be thou exalted , O God , above the heavens : let thy
glory be above all the earth.

## June 13

Psalm 89 : 11

The heavens are thine , the earth also is thine : as for the world
and the fulness thereof ,thou hast founded them.

Psalm 89 : 14

Justice and judgment are the habitation of thy throne : mercy and
truth shall go before thy face.

Psalm 89 : 15

Blessed is the people that know the joyful sound : they shall walk
, O LORD , in the light of thy countenance.

Isaiah 31 : 5

As birds flying , so will the LORD of hosts defend Jerusalem ;
defending also he will  deliver it ; and passing over he will
preserve it.

## June 14

Isaiah 33 : 17 - 21

(17)Thine eyes shall see the king in his beauty : they shall behold
the and that is very far off.

(18)Thine heart shall meditate terror .Where is the scribe ? Where
is the receiver ? Where is he that counted the towers?

(19)Thou shall not see a fierce people , a people of a deeper
speech than thou canst perceive ; of a stammering
tongue , that thou canst not understand .

(20)Look upon Zion , the city of our solemnities : thine eyes shall
see Jerusalem a quiet habitation , a tabernacle that shall not be
taken down ; not one of the stakes thereof shall ever be removed

, neither shall any  of the cords thereof be broken .

(21)But their the glorious LORD will be unto us a place of broad rivers and streams ; wherein shall go no galley with oars , neither shall gallant ship pass thereby .

Isaiah 59 : 2 -4

(2)But their iniquities have separated between you and your God , and your sins have hid his face from you , that he will not hear.

(3)For your hands are defiled with blood , and your fingers with iniquity ; your lips have spoken lies , your  tongue hath muttered perverseness.

(4)None calleth for justice , nor any pleadeth for truth : they trust in vanity , and speak lies ; they conceive mischief , and bring forth iniquity.

Isaiah 60 : 1

Arise , shine ; for thy light is come , and the glory of the LORD is risen upon thee.

Isaiah 59 : 1

Behold , the LORD'S hand is not shortened , that it cannot save ; neither his ear heavy , that it cannot hear:

## June 15

Psalm 85 : 1- 2

(1)To the chief Musician , A Psalm  for the sons of Korah . LORD , thou hast been favourable unto thy land : thou hast brought back the captivity of Jacob.

(2)Thou hast forgiven  the iniquity of thy people , thou hast covered all their sin.

Job 4 : 10

The roaring of the lion , and the voice of the fierce lion , and the teeth of the young lions , are broken .

Psalm 143 : 4 -12

(4)Therefore is my spirit overwhelmed within me ; my heart within me is desolate.

(5)I remember the days of old ; I meditate on all thy works ; I muse on the work of thy hands.

(6)I stretch forth my hands unto thee : my soul thirsteth after thee , as a thirsty land. Selah .

(7)Hear me speedily , O LORD : my spirit faileth : hide not thy face from me , lest I be like unto them that go down into the pit.

(8)Cause me to hear thy lovingkindness in the morning ; for in thee do I trust : cause me to know the way wherein I should walk ; for I lift up my soul unto thee.

(9)Deliver me , O LORD , from mine enemies : I flee unto thee to hide me.

(10)Teach me to do thy will ; for thou art my God : thy spirit is good ; lead me into the land of uprightness.

(11)Quicken me , O LORD , for thy name's sake : for thy righteousness sake bring my soul out of trouble.

(12)And of thy mercy cut off mine enemies , and destroy all them that afflict my soul : for I am thy servant.

Psalm 102 : 13 -14

(13)Thou shalt arise , and have mercy upon Zion : for the time to favour her , yea , the set time , is come.

(14)For thy servants take pleasure in her stones , and favour the dust thereof.

## June 17

Psalm 103 : 13

Like as a father pitieth his children , so the LORD pitieth them that fear him.

Psalm 102 : 12

But thou , O LORD , shalt endure for ever ; and thy remembrance unto all generations .

Zephaniah 3 : 12 -17

(12)I will also leave in the midst of thee an afflicted and poor people , and they shall trust in the name of the LORD.

(13The remnant of Israel shall not do iniquity , nor speak lies ; neither shall a deceitful tongue be found in their mouth : for they shall feed and lie down , and none shall make them afraid.

(14)Sing , O daughter of Zion ; shout , O Israel ; be glad and rejoice with all the heart , O daughter of Jerusalem.

(15)The LORD hath taken away thy judgments , he hath cast out thine enemy : the king of Israel , even the LORD , is in the midst of thee : thou shalt not see evil any more.

(16)In that day it shall be said to Jerusalem , Fear thou not : and to Zion , Let not thine hands be slack.

(17)The LORD thy God in the midst of thee is mighty ; he will save, he will rejoice over thee with joy ; he will rest in his love , he will joy over thee with singing.`

## June 18

Psalm 113 : 1

Praise ye the LORD . Praise , O ye servants of the LORD , praise the name of the LORD.

Mark 11 : 24

Therefore I say unto you , What things soever ye desire , when ye pray , believe that ye receive them , and ye shall have them.

## June 19

Psalm 40 : 13
Be pleased , O LORD , to deliver me : O LORD , make haste to help me.
Isaiah 59 :4
None calleth for justice , nor any pleaded for truth : they trust in vanity , and speak lies ; they conceive mischief , and bring forth iniquity ,
Isaiah 60 : 1
Arise , shine ; for thy light is come , and the glory of the LORD is risen upon thee.

## June 20

Hebrews 1 : 13
But to which of the angels said he at any time , Sit on my right hand , until I make thine enemies thy footstool ?
Psalm 126 : 5
They that sow in tears shall reap in joy .

## June 21

Psalm 125 : 1
A Song of degrees . They that trust in the LORD shall be as mount Zion , which cannot be removed , but abideth for  ever.
Psalm 68 : 11
The Lord gave the word : great was the company of those that published it.

## June 22

Psalm 56 : 11
In God have I put my trust : I will not be afraid  what man can do

unto me .

Psalm 59 : 17

Unto thee , O my strength , will I sing : for God is my defence , and the God of my mercy.

Psalm 66 : 1

To the chief Musician , A Song or Psalm . Make a joyful noise unto the God , all ye lands :

Psalm 66 : 20

Blessed be God , which hath not turned away my prayer , nor his mercy from me.

## June 23

Psalm 66 : 20

Blessed be God , which hath not turned away my prayer , nor his mercy from me.

Psalm 68 : 19

Blessed be the  Lord , who daily loadeth us with benefits , even the God of our salvation .

Psalm 128 : 2

For thou shalt eat the labour of thine hands : happy shalt thou be , and it shall be well with thee.

## June 24

Psalm 135 : 4

For the LORD hath chosen Jacob unto himself , and Israel for his peculiar treasure .

Psalm 50 : 23

Whoso offereth  praise glorifieth  me : and to him that ordered his conversation aright will I shew  the salvation of God .

## June 25

Psalm 50 : 23

Whoso offereth praise glorifieth me : and to him that ordered his conversation aright will I shew the salvation of God .

Psalm 51 : 1

To the chief Musican , A Psalm of David , when Nathan the prophet came unto him , after he had gone in to Bathsheba .

Have mercy upon me , O God , according to thy lovingkindness : according unto the multitude of thy tender mercies blot out my transgressions.

Proverbs 3 : 5 -6

(5)Trust in the LORD with all thine heart ; and lean not unto thine own understanding.

(6)In all thy ways acknowledge him , and he shall direct thy paths .

## June 26

Psalm 89 : 8

O LORD God of hosts , who is a strong LORD like unto thee? Or to thy faithfulness round about thee?

Psalm 40 : 13

Be pleased , O LORD , to deliver me : O LORD , make haste to help me .

## June 27

Psalm 51 : 7

Purge me with hyssop , and I shall be clean : wash me , and I shall be whiter than snow.

Psalm 51 : 10

Create in me a clean heart , O God ; and renew a right spirit within me .

Psalm 51 : 8

Make me to hear joy and gladness ; that the bones which thou

hast broken may rejoice .
Psalm 128 : 2
For thou shalt eat the labour of thine hands : happy shalt thou be
, and it shall well with thee .

## June 28

Psalm 135 : 4 For the LORD hath chosen Jacob unto himself , and
Israel for his peculiar treasure .
Psalm 135 : 1
Praise ye the LORD , Praise ye the name of the LORD : praise
him , O ye servants of the LORD.

## June 29

Psalm 132 : 1
A Song of degrees . LORD , remember David , and all his
afflictions.
Psalm `131 : 1
A Song of degrees of  David . LORD , my heart is not haughty ,
nor mine eyes lofty : neither do I exercise myself in great matters
, or in things too high for me .
Psalm 128 : 2
For thou shalt eat the labour of thine hands: happy shalt thou be ,
and it shall be well with thee.
Psalm 131 : 1
A Song of degrees of  David . LORD , my heart is not haughty ,
nor mine eyes lofty : neither do I exercise myself  in great matters
, or in things too high for me .
Psalm 132 : 1
A Song of degrees . LORD , remember David , and all his
afflictions :

# June 30

Psalm 12 : 7

Thou shalt keep them , O LOD , thou shalt preserve them from this generation for ever.

## July 1

Psalm 17 : 15
As for me I will behold thy face in righteousness : I shall be
satisfied , when I awake , with thy likeness.
Psalm 51 : 1
To the chief Musician , A Psalm of David , when Nathan the
prophet came unto him , after he had gone in to
Bathsheba. Have mercy upon me , O God , according to thy
lovingkindness : according unto the multitude of thy
tender mercies blot out my transgressions.

## July 2

Psalm 50 : 23
Whoso offered praise glorifieth me : and to him that ordered his
conversation aright will I shew the salvation of God.
Psalm 106 : 4
Remember me , O LORD , with the favour that thou bearest unto
thy people : O visit me with thy salvation ;

## July 3

Psalm 106 : 1
Praise ye the LORD . O give thanks unto the LORD ; for he is
good : for his mercy endureth  for ever.
Psalm 104 : 2
Who coverest thyself with light as with a garment : who
stretchest out the heavens like a curtain :
Psalm 128 : 2
For thou shalt eat the labour of thine hands : happy shalt thou be
, and it shall be well with thee.

## July 4

Psalm 135 : 4
For the LORD hath chosen Jacob unto himself , and Israel for his peculiar treasure .
Malachi 3 : 17
And they shall be mine , saith the LORD of hosts , in that day when I make up my jewels ; ad I will spare them , as
a man spareth his own son that serveth him.
Psalm 104 : 27
These wait all upon thee ; that thou mayest give them their meat in due season .

## July 5

Psalm 135 : 4
For the LORD hath chosen Jacob unto himself , and Israel for his peculiar treasure.
Psalm 67 : 5 -7
(5)Let the people praise thee , O God ; let all the people praise thee.
(6)Then shall the earth yield her increase ; and God , even our own God , shall bless us .
(7)Godshall bless us ; and all the ends of the earth shall fear him.

## July 6

Psalm 65 : 9
Thou visitest the earth , and waterest it : thou greatly enrichest it with the river of God , which is full of water : thou prepares them corn , when thou hast so provided for it .
Psalm 66 : 8
O bless our soul in life , and suffered not our feet to be moved .

Psalm 51 : 19

Then shalt thou be pleased with the sacrifices of righteousness ,
with burnt offering and whole burnt offering : then shall they
offer bullocks upon thine altar.

Psalm 4 : 5

Offer the sacrifices of righteousness , and put your trust in the
LORD .

## July 7

Psalm 5: 3

My voice shalt thou hear in the morning , O LORD ; in the
morning will I direct my prayer unto thee , and will look up .

Psalm 73 : 9

They set their mouth against the heavens , and their tongue
walketh through the earth .

Psalm 73 : 17

Until I went into the sanctuary  of God ; then understood I their
end.

Psalm 73 : 1

A Psalm of Israel , even to such as are of a clean heart.

## July 8

Psalm 72 : 8

He shall have dominion also from the river unto the ns of the
earth .

2 Chronicles 7 : 14

For if I have boasted any thing to him of you , I am not ashamed ;
but as we spake all things to you in truth , even so our boasting ,
which I made before Titus , is found a truth .

# July 9

Nehemiah 7 : 5 - 6

(5)And my God put into mine heart to gather together the nobles , and the rulers , and the people , that they might be reckoned by genealogy .And I found a register of the genealogy of them which came up at the first , and found written therein ,
(6)These are the children of the province , that went up out of the captivity , of those that had ben carried away , whom Nebuchadnezzar the king of Babylon had carried away , and came again to Jerusalem and to Judah , every one unto his city ;

Psalm 27 : 4

One thing have I desired of the LORD , that will I seek after ; that I may dwell in the house of the LORD all the days of my life , to behold the beauty of the LORD , and to inquire in his temple .

Luke 1: 28

And the angel came in unto her , and said , Hail , thou that art highly favored , the Lord is with thee : blessed art thou among women .

# July 10

Job 39 : 1

Knowest thou the time when the wild goats of the rock bring forth ? Or canst thou mark when the hinds do calve?

Psalm 73 : 17-18

(17)Until I went into the sanctuary of God ; then understood I their end.
(18)Surely thou didst set them in slippery places  thou castedst them down into destruction .

Psalm 73 : 1

A Psalm of ASAP . Truly God is good to Israel , even to sch as are of a clean heart .

Psalm 119 : 15 -16

(15)I will meditate in thy precepts , and have respect unto thy ways .

(16)I will delight myself in thy statutes : I will not forget thy word.

## July 11

Psalm 118 : 1

O give thanks unto the LORD ; for he is good : because his mercy endureth for ever .

Jeremiah 21 : 11

And touching the house of the king of Judah , say , Hear ye the word of the LORD ;

Psalm 108 : 1

A Song or Psalm of David . O God , my heart is fixed ; I will sing and give praise , even with my glory .

## July 12

Psalm 110 : 1

A Psalm of David . The LORD said unto my Lord , Sit thou at my right hand , until I make thine enemies thy footstool .

Psalm 118 : 27

God is the LORD , which hath shewed us light : bind the sacrifice with cords , even unto the horns of the altar.

Nehemiah 6 : 9

For they all made us afraid , saying , Their hands shall be weakened from the work , that it be not done. Now therefore , O God , strengthen my hands .

Nehemiah 6 : 15

So the wall was finished in the twenty and fifth day of the month

Elul , in fifty and two days .

## July 13

Psalm 108 : 1
A Song or Psalm of David . O God , my heart is fixed ; I
will sing and give praise , even with my glory .
Psalm 109 : 1
To the chief Musician , A Psalm of David . Hold not thy peace , O
God of my praise ;
Psalm 110 : 1
A Psalm of David . The LORD said unto my Lord , Sit thou at my
right hand , until I make thine enemies thy footstool.

## July 14

Psalm 110 : 2 - 3
(2)The LORD shall send the rod of the strength out of Zion : rule
thou in the midst of thine enemies.
(3)Thy people shall be willing in the day of thy power , in the
beauties of holiness from the womb of the morning : thou hast
the dew of thy youth.
Psalm 109 : 21
But do thou for me , O GOD the Lord , for thy name's sake :
because thy mercy is good , deliver thou me .
I Corinthians 15 : 58
Therefore , my beloved brethen , be ye steadfast , unmovable ,
always abounding in the work of the Lord , forasmuch as ye
know that your labour is not in vain in the Lord .

## July 15

Psalm 128 : 2
For thou shalt eat the labour of thine hands : happy shalt thou be

, and it shall be well with thee.

Psalm 134 : 1

A Song of degrees . Behold , bless ye the LORD , all ye servants of the LORD , which by night stand in the house of the LORD.

Psalm 128 : 4

Behold , that thus shall the man be blessed that feared the LORD.

## July 16

Psalm 135 : 6

Whatsoever the LORD pleased , that did he in heaven , and in earth , in the seas , and all deep places.

Psalm 135 : 1- 6

(1)Praise ye the LORD . Praise ye the name of the LORD ; praise him , O ye servants of the LORD.

(2)Ye that stand in the house of the LORD , in the courts of the house of our God,

(3)Praise the LORD ; for the LORD is good : sing praises unto his name ; for it is pleasant.

(4)For the LORD hath chosen Jacob unto himself , and Israel for his peculiar treasure.

(5)For I know that the LORD is great , and that our Lord is above all gods.

(6)Whatsoever the LORD pleased , that did he in heaven , and in earth , in the seas , and all deep places.

## July 17

Psalm 117 : 1

Praise the LORD , all ye nations : praise him , all ye people .

Psalm 128 : 2

For thou shalt eat the labour of thine hands; happy shalt thou be , and it shall be well with thee.

## July 18

Psalm 132 : 1

A Song of degrees .LORD , remember David , and all his afflictions .

Psalm 119 : 25

DALETH . My soul cleaveth unto the dust : quicken thou me according to thy word .

Psalm 119 : 27

Make me to understand the way of thy precepts : so shall I talk of thy wondrous works.

Psalm134 : 1- 3

(1)A Song of degrees . Behold , bless ye the LORD , all ye servants of the LORD , which by night stand in the house of the LORD .

(2)Lift up your hands in the sanctuary , and bless the LORD .

(3)The LORD that made heaven and earth bless thee out of Zion.

Psalm 132 : 13 - 15

(13)For the LORD hath chosen Zion ; he hath desired it for his habitation.

(14)This is my rest for ever : here will I dwell ; for I have desired it .

(15)I will abundantly bless her provision : I will satisfy her poor with bread .

## July 19

Psalm 132 : 12

If thy children will keep my covenant and my testimony that I shall teach them , their children shall also sit upon thy throne for evermore .

Psalm 115 : 1

Not unto us , O LORD , not unto us , but unto thy name give glory , for thy mercy , and for thy truth's sake .

Psalm 121 : 1 -2

(1)A Song of degrees . I will lift up mine eyes unto the hill , from whence cometh my help.

(2)My help cometh from the LORD , which made heaven and earth .

## July 20

Psalm 119 : 175

Let my soul live , and it shall praise thee ; and let thy judgments help me .

Psalm 17 : 15

As for me , I will behold thy face in righteousness : I shall be satisfied , when I awake , with thy likeness .

## July 21

Job 8 : 7

Though thy beginning was small , yet thy latte end should greatly increase .

Psalm 128 : 2

For thou shalt eat the labour of thine hands : happy shalt thou be , and it shall be well with thee.

## July 22

Psalm 135 : 4

For the LORD hath chosen Jacob unto himself , and Israel for his peculiar treasure .

Psalm 128 : 2

For thou shalt eat the labour of thine hands : happy shalt thou be , and it shall be well with thee.

# July 23

Psalm 102 : 1
A Prayer of the afflicted , when he is overwhelmed , and poureth out his complaint before the LORD , Hear my prayer , O LORD , and let my cry come unto thee .

Psalm 19 : 1 - 6
(1)To the chief Musician , A Psalm of David . The heavens declare the glory of God ; and the firmament sheweth his handiwork.
(2)Day unto day uttered speech , and night unto night sheweth knowledge.
(3)there is no speech nor language , where their voice is not heard .
(4)Their line is gone out through all the earth , and their words to the end of the world .In them hath he set a tabernacle for the sun
(5)Which is as a bridegroom coming out of his chamber ,
and rejoiceth as a strong man to run a race.
(6)His going forth is from the end of the heaven , and his circuit unto the ends of it : and there is nothing hid from the heat thereof .

# July 24

Psalm 18 : 32
It is God that girdeth me with strength , and maketh my way perfect.

Psalm 128 : 2
For thou shalt eat the labour of thine hands : happy shalt thou be , and it shall be well with thee.

## July 25

Psalm 135 : 6
Whatsoever the LORD pleased , that did he in heaven , and in earth , in the seas , and all deep places.
Psalm 17 : 8
Keep me as the apple of the eye , hide me under the shadow of thy wings,

## July 26

Psalm 17 : 15
As for me , I will behold thy face in righteousness : I will behold thy face in righteousness : I shall be satisfied , when I awake , with thy likeness .
Psalm 18 : 1- 2
(1)To the chief Musician , A Psalm of David , the servant of the LORD , who spake unto the LORD the words of this song in the day that the LORD delivered him from the hand of all his enemies , and from the hand of Saul : And he said , I will love thee , O LORD , my strength .
 (2)The LORD is my rock , and my fortress , and my deliverer ; my God , my strength , on whom I will trust ; my buckler , and the horn of my salvation , and my high tower .
Psalm 16 : 1
Michtam of David . Preserve me , O God : for in thee do I put my trust .
Psalm 134 : 1 - 3
(1)A Song of degrees . Behold , bless ye the LORD , all ye servants of the LORD , which by night stand in the house of the LORD.
(2)Lift up your hands in the sanctuary , and bless the LORD .
(3)The LORD that made heaven and earth bless thee out of Zion .

# July 27

Psalm 71 : 14

But I will hope continually , and will yet praise thee more and more .

Psalm 11 : 1 -4

(1)TO the chief Musician , A Psalm of David . In the LORD put I my trust : how say ye to my soul , Flee as a bird to your mountain ?

(2)For , lo , the wicked bend their bow , they make ready their arrow upon the string , that they may privily shoot at the upright in heart.

(3)If the foundations be destroyed , what can the righteous do?

(4)The LORD is in his holy temple , the LORD'S throne is in heaven : his eyes behold , his eyelids try , the children of men.

# July 28

Psalm 8 : 9

O LORD our Lord , how excellent is thy name in all the earth!

Psalm 11 : 1

To the chief Musician , A Psalm of David .In the LORD put I my trust : how say ye to my soul , Flee as a bird to your mountain ?

Psalm 12 : 1

To the chief Musician upon Sheminith , A Psalm of David . Help , LORD ; for the godly man ceaseth; for the faithful fail from among the children of men .

Psalm 9 : 1

To the chief Musician upon Muthlabben , A Psalm of David . I will praise thee , O LORD , with my whole heart ; I will shew forth all thy marvelous works .

## July 29

Psalm 11 : 4
The LORD is in his holy temple , the LORD'S throne is in heaven
: his eyes behold , his eyelids try , the children of men .
Psalm 56 : 11
In God have I put my trust : I will not be afraid what man can do
unto me.
Psalm 59 : 17
Unto thee , O my strength , will I sing : for God is my defence ,
and the God of my mercy.
Matthew 7 : 7
Ask , and it shall be given you ; seek , and ye shall find ; knock ,
and it shall be opened unto you :

## July 30

Ecclesiastes 2 : 15 - 26
(15)Then said I in my heart , As it happeneth to the fool , so it
happeneth even to me ; and why was I then more
wise ? Then I said in my heart , that this also is vanity .
(16)For there is no rememberance of the wise more than of the
fool for ever  seeing that which now is in the days to come shall
all be forgotten .,And how dieth the wise man ? As the fool.
(17)Therefore I hated life ; because the work that is wrought
under the sun is grievous unto me : for all is vanity and vexation
of spirit .
(18)Yea , I hated all my labour which I had taken under the sun :
because I should leave it unto the man that shall be after me .
(19)And who knoweth whether he shall be a wise man or a fool ?
Yet shall he have rule over all my labour wherein I have
laboured , and wherein I have shewed myself wise under the

sun. This is also vanity .

(20)Therefore I went about to cause my heat to despair of all the labour which I took under the sun .

(21)For there is a man whose labour is in wisdom , and in knowledge , and in equity ; yet to a man that hath not laboured therein shall he leave it for his portion .

(22)for what hath man of all his labour , and of he vexation of his heart , wherein he hath laboured under the sun ?

(23)For all his days are sorrows , and his travail grief ; yea , his heart taketh not rest in the night .This is also vanity .

(24)There is nothing better for a man , than that he should eat and drink , and that he should make his soul enjoy good in his labour .This also I saw , that it was from the hand of God.

(25)For who can eat , or who else can hasten hereunto , more than I ?

(26)For God giveth to a man that is good in his sight wisdom , and knowledge , and joy : but to the sinner he giveth travail , to gather and to heap up , that he may give to him that is vanity and vexation of spirit.

Psalm 31 : 24

Be of good courage , and he shall strengthen your heart , all ye that hope in the LORD .

Psalm 128 : 2

For thou shalt eat the labour of thine hands : happy shalt thou be , and it shall be well with thee .

## July 31

Psalm 66 : 1

To the chief Musician , A Song or Psalm . Make a joyful noise unto God , all ye lands :

Psalm 68 : 19

Blessed be the Lord , who daily loadeth us with benefits , even the God of our salvation .

Psalm 143 : 4- 8

(4)Therefore is my spirit overwhelmed within me ; my heart within me is desolate .

(5)I remember the days of old ; I meditate on all thy works ; I muse on the work of thy hands .

(6)I stretch forth my hands unto thee : my soul thirsteth after thee , as a thirsty land . Selah .

(7)hear me speedily , O LORD : my spirit faileth : hide not thy face from me , lest I be like unto them that go down into the pit.

(8)Cause me to hear thy lovingkindness in the morning ; for in thee do I trust : cause me to know the way wherein I should walk ; for I lift up my soul unto thee.

## August 1

Psalm 97 : 4

His  lightnings enlightened the world : the earth saw , and
trembled .

Psalm 102 : 1

A Prayer of the afflicted , when he is overwhelmed , and
poureth out his complaint before the LORD . Hear my prayer , O
LORD ,and let my cry come unto thee.

## August  2

Psalm 31 : 14

Pull me out of the net that they have laid privily for me : for thou
art my strength .

Psalm 69 : 35

For God will save Zion , and will build the cities of Judah : that
they may dwell there , and have it in possession .

## August 3

Psalm 69 : 35

For God will save Zion , and will build the cities of Judah : that
they may dwell there , and have it in possession .

Psalm 68 : 29

Because of thy temple at Jerusalem shall kings bring presents
unto thee .

Psalm 71 : 1

In thee , O LORD , do I put my trust : let me never be put to
confusion .

## August 4

Psalm 68 : 31

Princess shall come out of Egypt ; Ethiopia shall soon stretch out her hands unto God .

Psalm 66 : 1

To the chief Musician , A Song or Psalm . Make a joyful noise unto God , all ye lands .

Psalm 31 : 14

But I trusted in thee , O LORD : I said , Thou art my God

Psalm 69 : 35

For god will save Zion , and will build  the cities of Judah : that they may dwell there , and have it in possession .

## August 5

Psalm 67 : 1

To the chief Musician on Neginoth , A Psalm or Song . God be merciful unto us , and bless us ; and cause his face to shine upon us ; Selah .

Psalm 71 : 1

In the , O LORD , do I put my trust : let me never be put to confusion .

## August 6

Nehemiah 6 : 15

So the wall was finished in the twenty and fifth day of the month Elul , in fifty and two days .

Psalm 17 :15

As for me , I will behold thy face in righteousness : I shall be satisfied , when I awake , with thy likeness.

Ezekiel 36 : 9 -11

(9)For , behold , I am for you , and I will turn unto you , and ye shall be tilled and sown :

(10)And I will multiply men upon you , all the house of Israel , even all of it : and the cities shall be inhabited , and the wastes shall be builded :

(11)And I will multiply upon you man and beast ; and they shall increase and bring fruit : and I will settle you after your old estates , and will do better unto you than at your beginnings : and ye shall know that I am the LORD.

## August 7

Ezekiel 36 : 36
Then the heathen that are left round about you shall know that I the LORD build the ruined places , and plant that that was desolate : I the LORD have spoken it , and I will do it .
Psalm 128 : 2
For thou shall eat the labour of thine hands : happy shalt thou be , and it shall be well with thee.

## August 8

Psalm 92 : 4
For thou , LORD , hast made me glad through thy work : I will triumph in the works of thy hands .
Psalm 47 : 6 -9
(6)Sing praises to God , sing praises : sing praises unto our King , sing praises .
(7)For God is the King of all the earth : sing ye praises with understanding .
(8)God reigneth over the heathen : God sitteth upon the throne of his holiness.
(9)The princes of the people are gathered together , even the people of the god of Abraham : for the shields of the earth belong unto God : he is greatly exalted .

## August 9

Psalm 45 : 1

To the chief Musician upon Shoshanna , for the sons of
Korah , Maschil , A Song of loves .My heart is inditing a good
thing which I have made touching the king: my tongue is the pen
of a ready writer.

Psalm 71 : 1- 4

(1)In thee , O LORD , do I put my trust : let me never be put to
confusion .

(2)Deliver me in they righteousness , and cause me to
escape : incline thine ear unto me , and save me .

(3)Be thou my strong habitaion , whereunto I  may continually
resort : thou hast given commandment to save me ; for  thou art
my rock and my fortress.

(4)Deliver me , O my God , out of the hand of the wicked , out of
the hand of the righteous and cruel man .

## August 10

Psalm 69 : 36

The seed also of his servants shall inherit it : and they that love
his name shall dwell therein .

Psalm 71 : 1

In thee , O LORD , do I put my trust : let me never be put to
confusion .

## August 11

Psalm 69 : 1

To the chief Musician upon Shoshanna , Psalm of David . Save
me , O God ; fodr the waters are come in unto my soul .

Psalm 69 : 6let not them that wait on thee , O Lord GOD of hosts
, ashamed for my sake : let not those that seek thee be
confounded for my sake , O God of Israel .

110

Psalm 69 : 5

O God , thou knowest my foolishness ; and my sins are
not hid from thee .

Psalm 72 : 1

A Psalm for Solomon . Give the king thy judgments , O God ,
and thy righteousness unto the king's son.

Psalm 73 : 1

A Psalm of ASAP . Truly God is good to Israel , even to such as
are of a clean heart .

## August 12

Psalm 71 : 14

But I will hope continually , and will yet praise thee more and
more .

Psalm 51 : 1

To the chief Musician , A Psalm of David , when Nathan the
prophet came unto him , after he had gone in to Bathsheba .
Have mercy upon me , O God , according to thy lovingkindness :
according unto the multitude  of thy mercies blot out my
transgressions.

## August 13

Psalm 49 : 1

To the chief Musician , A Psalm for the sons of Korah . Hear this ,
all ye people ; give ear , all ye inhabitants of the world :

Psalm 50 : 1

A Psalm of ASAP . The mighty God , even the LORD ,hath
spoken , and called the earth  from the rising of the sun unto the
going down thereof .

Psalm 51 : 10

Create in me a clean heart , O God ; and renew a right spirit
within me .

Psalm 27 : 14

Wait on the LORD : be of good courage , and he shall strengthen thine heart : wait , I say , on the LORD.

## August 14

Psalm 27 : 1

A Psalm of David . The LORD is my light and my salvation ; whom shall I fear ? The LORD is the strength of my life ; of whom shall I be afraid ?

Psalm 80 : 3

Turn us again , O God , and cause thy face to shine ; and we shall be saved .

Psalm 80 : 19

Turn us again , O LORD God of hosts , cause thy face to shine ; and we shall be saved .

## August 15

Psalm 80 : 17

Let thy and be upon the man of thy right hand , upon the son of man whom thou madest strong for thyself .

Psalm 128 : 2

For thou shalt eat the labour of thine hands : happy shalt thou be , and it shall be well with thee.

## August 16

Psalm 128 : 3 -6

(3)Thy wife shall be as a fruitful vine be the sides of thine house : thy children like olive plants round about thy table .

(4)Behold , that thus shall the man be blessed that feareth the LORD .

(5)The LORD shall bless thee out of Zion : and thou shalt see the good of Jerusalem all the days of thy life .

(6)Yea , thou shalt see thy children's children ,and peace upon Israel .

Psalm 128 : 2

For thou shalt eat the labour of thine hands : happy shalt thou be , and it shall be well with thee .

## August 17

Psalm 133 : 1

A Song of degrees of David . Behold , how good and how pleasant it is for brethren to dwell together in unity !

Psalm 111 : 1

Praise ye the LORD . I will praise the LORD with my whole heart , in the assembly of the upright , and in the congregation .

Psalm 117 : 1 - 2

(1)O Praise the LORD , all ye nations : praise him , all ye people .

(2)For his merciful kindness is great toward us; and the truth of the LORD endureth for ever . Praise ye the LORD .

## August 18

Psalm 119 : 17

GIMEL . Deal bountiful with thy servant , that I may live , and keep thy word .

Isaiah 60 : 13

The glory of Lebanon shall come unto thee , the fir tree , the pine tree , and the box together , to beautify the place

of my sanctuary ; and I will make the place of my feet glorious .

## August 19

Psalm 51 : 12
Restore unto me the joy of thy salvation ; and uphold me with
thy free spirit.
Psalm 50 : 23
Whoso offered praise glorifieth me : and to him that ordered his
conservation aright will I shew the salvation of God.

## August 20

Psalm 50 : 1 - 4
(1)A Psalm of Asaph . The mighty God , even the LORD ,hath
spoken ,and called the earth from the rising of the sun unto the
going down thereof .
(2)Out of Zion , the perfection of beauty , God hath shined.
(3)Our God shall come , and shall not keep silence : a fire shall
not keep silence : a fire shall devour before him ,and it shall be
very tempestuous round about him .
(4)He shall call to the heavens from above , and to the earth , that
he may judge his people.
John 1 : 12
But as many as received him  to them gave he power to become
the sons of God , even to them that believe on his name :
Isaiah 6 : 4
And the post of the door moved at the voice of him that cried ,
and the house was filled with smoke .
Psalm 8 : 2
Out of the mouth of babes and sucklings hast thou
ordained strength because of thine enemies , that thou mightest
still the enemy and the avenger.

## August 21

Psalm 89 : 28
My mercy will I keep for him for evermore , and my covenant
shall stand fast with him.
Psalm 8 : 9
O LORD our Lord , how excellent is thy name in all the earth.

## August 22

Psalm 11 : 1
To the chief Musician , A Psalm of David . In the LORD put I my
trust : how say ye to my soul , Flee as a bird to your mountain .
Psalm 119 : 105
NUN , Thy word is a lamp unto my feet , and a light unto my
path.

## August 23

Psalm 119 : 45
And I will walk at liberty : for I seek thy precepts.
Psalm 78 : 42
They remembered not his hand , nor the day when he delivered
them from the enemy .
Psalm 8 : 2
Out of the mouth of babes and sucklings hast thou ordained
strength because of thine enemies , that thou mightest still the
enemy and the avenger.

## August 24

Psalm 11 : 1
To the chief Musician , A Psalm of David . In the LORD put I my
trust : how say ye to my soul , Flee as a bird to your mountain.

Psalm 128 : 2
For thou shalt eat the labour of thine hands : happy shalt thou be , and it shall be well with thee .

## August 25

Psalm 57 : 1
To the chief Musician , Altaschith , Michtam of David , when he fed from Saul in the cave .Be merciful uto  me , O God , be merciful unto me  for my soul trusteth in thee : yea , in the shadow of thy wings will I make my refuge , until these calamities be overpast .
Psalm 128 : 2
For thou shalt eat the labour of thine hands : happy shalt thou be , and it shall be well with thee.
Psalm 40 : 1
To the chief Musician , A Psalm of David . I waited patiently for the LORD ; and he inclined unto me , and heard my cry .

## August 26

Psalm 37 : 28
For the LORD loveth judgement , and forsaketh not his saints ; they are preserved for ever : but the seed of the wicked shall be cut off .
Psalm 37 : 34
Wait on the LORD , and keep his way , and he shall exalt thee to inherit the land : when the wicked are cut off , thou shalt see it .
Palm 119 : 101
I have refrained my feet from every evil way , that I might keep thy word.
Psalm 119 : 105
NUN .Thy word is a lamp unto my feet , and a light unto my path.
**116**

## August 27

Psalm 89 : 15

Blessed is the people that know the joyful sound : they shall walk , O LORD , in the light of thy countenance.

Psalm 87 : 4 - 5

(4)I will make mention of Rahab and Babylon to them that know me : behold Philistia , and Tyre , with Ethiopia ; this man was born there .

(5)And of Zion it shall be said , This and that man was born in he : and the highest himself shall establish her .

## August 28

Psalm 88 : 1

A Song or Psalm for the sons of Korah , to the chief Musician upon Mahalath Leannoth , Maschil of Heman the Ezrahite . O LORD God of my salvation , I have cried day and night before thee:

Psalm 80 : 17

Let thy hand be upon the man of thy right hand , upon the son of man whom thou madest strong for thyself .

## August 29

Psalm 78 : 72

So he fed them according to the integrity of his heart ; and guided them by the skilfulness of his hands .

Isaiah 29 : 23 - 24

(23)But when he seeth his children , the work of mine hands , in the midst of him , they shall sanctify my name , and sanctify the holy One of Jacob , and shall fear the God of Israel .

(24)They also that erred in spirit shall come to understanding , and they that murmured shall learn doctrine.

## August 30

Psalm 89 : 15
Blessed is the people that know the joyful sound : they
shall walk , O LORD , in the light of thy countenance.
Psalm 118 : 5
I called upon the LORD in distress : the LORD answered me ,
and set me in a large place.
 Psalm 117 : 2
For his merciful kindness is great toward us :  and the truth of
the LORD endureth for ever. Praise ye the LORD.

## August 31

Psalm 118 : 1
O give thanks unto the LORD ; for he is good : because his mercy
endureth for ever .
Psalm 118 : 5
I called upon the LORD in distress : the LORD answered
me , and set me in a large place.
Psalm 44 : 26
Arise for our help , and redeem us for thy mercies sake.

## September 1

Psalm 48 : 1
A Song and Psalm for the sons of Korah . Great is the LORD ,
and greatly to be praised in the city of our God , in the mountain
of his holiness.
Psalm 46 : 10
Be still , and know that I am God : I will be exalted among the
heathen , I will be exalted in the earth.
Psalm 46 : 5
God is in the midst of her ; she shall not be moved : God shall
help her , and that right early.
Psalm 31 : 14
But I trusted in thee , O LORD : I said , Thou art my God

## September 2

Psalm 59 : 17
Unto thee , O my strength , will I sing : for God is my defence ,
and the God of my mercy.
Psalm 119 : 52
I remembered  thy judgments of old , O LORD ; and have
comforted myself.

## September 3

Psalm 119 : 80 - 90
(80)Let my heart be sound in thy statutes ; that I be not ashamed .
(81)CAPH . My soul fainteth for thy salvation : but I
hope in thy word.
(82)Mine eyes fail for thy word, saying , when wilt thou comfort
me ?

(83)For I am become like a bottle in the smoke ; yet do I not forget thy statutes.

(84)How many are the days of thy servant ? When wilt thou execute judgement on them that persecute me ?

(85)The proud have digged pits for me , which are not after thy law.

(86)All thy commandments are faithful : they persecute me wrongly ; help thou me.

(87)They had almost consumed me upon earth ; but I forsook not thy precepts.

(88)Quicken me after thy lovingkindness ; so shall I keep the testimony of thy mouth.

(89)LAMED . For ever , O LORD , thy word is settled in heaven.

(90)Thy faithfulness is unto all generations : thou hast established the earth , and it abideth.

Psalm 89 : 14 - 15

(14)Justice and judgement are the habitation of thy throne : mercy and truth shall go before thy face.

(15)Blessed is the people that know the joyful sound : they shall walk , O LORD , in the light of thy countenance.

## September 4

Psalm 59 : 15

Let them wander up and down for meat , and grudge if they be not satisfied.

Psalm 128 : 2

For thou shalt eat the labour of thine hands : happy shalt thou be , and it shall be well with thee.

## September 5

Proverbs 17 : 22
A merry heart doeth good like a medicine : but a broken spirit drieth the bones.

Proverbs 16 : 21
The wise in heart shall be called prudent : and the sweetness of the lips increaseth learning .

Psalm 32 : 1
A Psalm of David, Maschil . Blessed is he whose transgression is forgiven , whose sin is covered .

Psalm 31 : 24
Be of a good courage , and he shall strengthen your heart , all that hope in the LORD.

Psalm 134 : 1 -2
(1)A Song of degrees . Behold , bless ye the LORD , all ye servants of the LORD , which by night stand in the house of the LORD.
(2)Lift up you hands in the sanctuary , and bless the LORD .

## September 6

Psalm 131 : 1- 3
(1)A Song of degrees of David . LORD , my heart is not haughty , nor mine eyes lofty : neither do I exercise myself in great matters , or in things too high for me .
(2)surely I have behaved and quieted myself , as a child that is weaned of his mother : my soul is even as a weaned child .
(3)Let Israel hope in the LORD from henceforth and for ever.

Isaiah 11: 2
And the spirit of the LORD shall rest upon him , the spirit of wisdom and understanding , the spirit of counsel and

might , the spirit of knowledge and of the fear of the LORD ;

## September 7

Psalm 3 : 7 - 8
(7)Arise , O LORD ; save me , O my God : for thou hast smitten all mine enemies upon the cheek bone ; thou hast broken the teeth of the ungodly .
(8)Salvation belonged unto the LORD : thy blessing is upon thy people . Selah .
Psalm 128 : 2
For shalt eat the labour of thine hands : happy shalt thou be , and it shall be well with thee.

## September 8

Psalm 116 : 1
I Live the LORD , because he hath heard my voice and my supplications.
Psalm 119 : 88 - 89
(88)Quicken me after thy lovingkindness ; so shall I keep the testimonies of thy mouth.
(89)LAMED . For ever , O LORD , thy word is settled in heaven.

## September 9

Psalm 107 : 22
And let them sacrifice the sacrifices of thanksgiving , and declare his works with rejoicing .
2 Chronicles 12 : 8
Nevertheless they shall be his servants ; that they My know my service , and the service of the kingdoms of the countries .

## September 10

Isaiah 2 : 21 22

(21)To go into the clefs of the rocks , and into the tops of the ragged rocks , for fear of the LORD , and for the glory of his majesty , when he ariseth to shake terribly the earth.

(22)Cease ye from man , whose breath is in his nostrils : for wherein is he to be accounted of ?

Ezekiel 9: 8

And it came to pass , while they were slaying them , and I was left , that I fell upon my face ,and cried ,and said , Ah Lord GOD ! Wilt thou destroy all the residue of Israel in thy pouring out of thy fury upon Jerusalem?

Psalm 128 : 2

For thou shalt eat the labour of thine hands : happy shalt thou be , and it shall be well with thee.

## September 11

Psalm 29 : 11

The LORD will give strength unto his people ; the LORD will bless his people with peace.

Psalm 31 : 14

But I trusted in thee , O LORD : I said , Thou art my God

Ezekiel 11: 19

And I will give them one heart , and I will put a new spirit within you ; and I will take the stony heart out of their flesh , and will give them an heart of flesh :

## September 12

Ester 5 : 2
And it was so , when the king saw Esther the queen standing in the court , that she obtained favour in his sight : and the king held out to Esther the golden sceptre that was in his hand . So Esther drew near , and touched the top of the sceptre .

Psalm 135 : 4- 6
(4)For the LORD hath chosen Jacob unto himself , and Israel for his peculiar treasure.
(5)For I know that the LORD is great , and that our LORD is above all gods.
(6)Whatesoever the LORD pleased , that did he in heaven , and in the earth , in the seas , and all deep places.

## September 13

Psalm 91 : 1
He that dwelleth in the secret place of the most High shall abide under the shadow of the Almighty .

Psalm 59 : 17
Unto thee , O my strength , will I sing : for God is my defence , and the God of my mercy.

## September 14

Job 5 : 15 -17
(15)But he saved the poor from the sword , from their mouth , and from the hand of the mighty .
(16)So the poor hath hope , and iniquity stoppeth her mouth .
(17)Behold , happy is the man whom God correcteth : therefore despise not thou the chastening of the Almighty

Psalm 55 : 23
But thou , O God , shalt bring them down into the pit of
destruction : bloody and deceitful men shall not live out half
their days ; but I will trust in thee.
Psalm 31 : 14
But I trusted in thee , O LORD : I said , Thou art my God .

## September 15

Psalm 65 : 1
To the chief Musician , A Psalm  and song of David . Praise
waited for thee , O God , in Sion : and unto thee shall the vow be
performed .
Psalm 64 : 10
The righteous shall be glad in the LORD , and shall trust in him ;
and all the upright in heart shall glory .
Psalm 68 : 11
The Lord gave the word : great was the company of those that
published it .
Psalm 68 : 19
Blessed be the Lord , who daily loadeth us with benefits , even
the God of our salvation . Selah .

## September 16

Psalm 37: 13
The Lord shall laugh at him : for he seeth that his day is coming.

## September 17

Psalm 37 : 4
Delight thyself also in the LORD ; and he shall give thee
the desires of thine heart .

Psalm 128 : 2
For thou shalt eat the labour of thine hands : happy shalt thou be
, and it shall be well with thee.

### September 18

Psalm 119 : 89
LAMED . For ever , O LORD , thy word is settled in heaven .
Psalm 31 : 14
But I trusted in thee , O  LORD : I said , Thou art my God .

### September 19

Psalm 29 : 11
The LORD will give strength unto his people ; the LORD will
bless people with peace.
Proverbs 25 : 2
It is the glory of God to conceal s thing : but the honour of kings
is to search out a matter .

### September 20

Psalm 119 : 105
Nun .Thy word is a lamp unto my feet ,and a light unto
my path .
Psalm 119 : 109
My soul is continually in my hand : yet do I not forget thy law .
John 16 : 13 - 15
(13)Howbeit when he , the Spirit of truth , is come , he will guide
you into all truth : for he shall not speak of himself ; but
whatsoever he shall hear , that shall he speak : and he shew you
things to come.

(14)He shall glorify me : for he shall receive of mine , and shall shew it unto you .

(15)All things that the Father hath he shall take of mine , and shall shew it unto you .

## September 21

Psalm 40 : 13
Be pleased , O LORD , to deliver me : O LORD , make haste to be ashamed and confounded together that seek after my soul to destroy it ; let them be driven backward and put to shame that wish me evil .

Psalm 128 : 2
For thou shalt eat the labour of thine hands : happy shalt thou be , and it shall be well with thee .

Psalm 135 : 4
For the LORD hath chosen Jacob unto himself , and Israel for his peculiar treasure .

## September 22

Psalm 101 : 6
We have sinned with our fathers , we have committed iniquity , we have done wickedly .

Proverbs 25 : 2
It is the glory of God to conceal a thing : but the honour of kings is to search out a matter .

## September 23

Psalm 40 : 13
Be pleased , O LORD , to deliver me : O LORD , make haste to help me .

Psalm 119 : 48

My hands also will I lift up unto thy commandments , which I have loved ; and I will meditate in thy statutes .

Palm 119 : 73

JOD . Thy hands have made me and fashioned me : give me understanding , that I may learn thy commandments .

## September 24

Psalm 119 : 71

It is good for that I have been afflicted ; that might learn thy statutes .

Psalm 31 : 24

Be of good courage , and he shall strengthen your heart , al ye that hope in the LORD .

2 Chronicles 7 : 14

If my people , which are called by my name , shall humble themselves , and pray , and seek my face , and turn from their wicked ways ; then will I hear from heaven , and will forgive their sin , and will heal their land .

## September 25

Psalm 59 : 17

Unto thee , O my strength , will I sing : for God is my defence , and the God of my mercy .

Psalm 134 : 1-2

(1)A Song of degrees .Behold , bless ye the LORD , all ye servants of the LORD ,which by night stand in the house of the LORD .
(2)Lift up your hands in the sanctuary , and bless the LORD .

## September 26

Psalm 128 : 2
For thou shalt eat the labour of thine hands : happy shalt thou be , and it shall be well with thee.
Psalm 119 : 145
KOPH . I cried with my whole heart ; hear me , O LORD : I will keep thy statutes .

## September 27

Psalm 51 : 10
Create in me a clean heart , O God ; and renew a right spirit within me .
Psalm 49 : 15
But God will redeem my soul from the power of the grave : for he shall receive me . Selah.
Psalm 135 : 4
For the LORD hath chosen Jacob unto himself , and Israel for his peculiar treasure .

## September 28

Psalm 134 : 3
The LORD that made heaven and earth bless thee  out of Zion .
Jeremiah 23 : 4
And I will set up shepherds over them which shall feed them : and they shall fear no more , nor be dismayed , neither shall they be lacking , saith the LORD .

## September 29

Jeremiah 23 : 3
And I will gather the remant of my flock out of all countries

whither I have driven them , and will bring them again to their folds ; and they shall be fruitful and increase .

Psalm 135 : 1- 6

(1)Praise ye the LORD . Praise ye the name of the LORD ; praise him , O ye servants of the LORD .

(2)Ye that stand in the house of the LORD , in the courts of the house of our God ,

(3)Praise the LORD ; for the LORD is good : sing  praises unto his name ; for it is pleasant .

(4)For the LORD hath chose Jacob unto himself , and Israel for his peculiar treasure .

(5)For I know that the LORD is great , and that our Lord is above all gods .

(6)Whatsoever the LORD pleased , that did he in heaven , and in earth , in the seas , and all deep places .

## September 30

Psalm 97 : 1

The LORD reigneth ; let the earth rejoice ; let the multitude of isles be glad thereof .

Psalm 102 : 1

A prayer of the afflicted , when he is overwhelmed , and poureth out his complaint before the LORD . Hear my prayer , O LORD , and let my cry come unto thee.

Psalm 102 : 12 - 13

(12)But thou , O LORD shalt endure for ever ; and thy remembrance unto all generations .

(13)Thou shalt arise , and have mercy upon Zion : for the time to favour her , yea , the set time , is come .

Psalm 134 : 1- 3

(1)A Song of degrees . Behold , bless ye the LORD , all ye servants of the LORD , which by night stand in the house of the

LORD

(2)Lift up your hands in the sanctuary , and bless the LORD .

(3)The LORD that made heaven and earth bless thee out of Zion .

Psalm 128 : 2

For thou shalt eat the labour of thine hands : happy shalt thou be , and it shall be well with thee.

Exodus 14 : 13

And Moses said unto the people , fear ye not , stand still , and see the salvation of the LORD , which he will shew to you to day : for the Egyptians whom ye have seen to day , ye shall shall see them  again no more for ever .

## October 1

Psalm 92 : 4
For thou , LORD , hast made me glad through thy work : I will triumph in the works of thy hands .
Psalm 93 : 1
The LORD reigneth , he is clothed with majesty ; the LORD is clothed with strength , wherewith he hath girded himself : the world also is established , that it cannot be moved.

## October 2

Psalm 94 : 1- 2
(1)O LORD God , to whom veangeance belonged ; O God , to whom vengeance belonged , shew thyself .
(2)Lift up thyself , thou judge of the earth : render a reward to the proud.
Psalm 128 : 2
For thou shalt eat the labour of thine hands : happy shalt thou be , and it shall be well with thee.

## October 3

Psalm 107 : 22
And let them sacrifice the sacrifices of thanksgiving , and declare his works with rejoicing .
Psalm 40 : 1
To the chief Musician , A Psalm of David . I waited patiently for the LORD : and he inclined unto me , and heard my cry .

## October 4

Psalm 27 : 1
A Psalm of David . The LORD is my light and my salvation ; whom shall I fear ? The LORD is the strength of my life ; of whom shall I be afraid.

## October 5

Matthew 18 : 10
Take heed that ye despise not one of these little ones ; for I say unto you , That in heaven their angels do always behold the face of my Father which is in heaven.
Psalm 23 : 5 -6
(5)Thou preparest a table before me in the presence of mine enemies : thou anointest my head with oil ; my cup runneth over .

(6)Surely goodness and mercy shall follow me all the days f my life : and I will dwell in the house of the LORD for ever .
Romans 8 : 6
For to be carnally minded is death ; but to be spiritually minded is life and peace.

## October 6

Psalm 24 : 7
Lift up your heads , O ye gates ; and be ye lift up , ye everlasting doors ; and the king of glory shall come in .
Psalm 128 : 2
For thou shalt eat the labour of thine hands : happy shalt thou be , and it shall be well with thee .

## October 7

Psalm 101 : 6
Mine eyes shall be upon the faithful of the land , that they may dwell with me : he that walketh in a perfect way , he shall serve me .
Psalm 8 : 9
O LORD our Lord , how excellent is thy name in all the earth !

## October 8

Psalm 11:1
To the chief Musician , A Psalm of David . In the LORD put I my trust : how say ye to my soul , Flee as a bird to your mountain ?

## October 9

Psalm 129 : 4
The LORD is righteous : he hath cut asunder the cords of the wicked .
Psalm 68 : 19
Blessed be the Lord , who daily loadeth us with benefits , even the God of our salvation . Selah .
Psalm 11 :1
To the chief Musician , A Psalm of David . In the LORD put I my trust : how say ye to  soul , Flee as a bird to your mountain ?
Psalm 8 : 6
Thou madest him to have dominion over the works of thy hands ; thou hast put all things under his feet :

## October 10

LORD , thou hast heard the desire of the humble : thou wilt prepare their heart , thou wilt cause thine ear to hear
Psalm 135 : 4
For the LORD hath chosen Jacob unto himself , and Israel for his peculiar treasure .

## October 11

Psalm 128 : 6
Yea , thou shalt see thy children's children , and peace upon Israel .
Psalm 128 : 5
The LORD shall bless thee out of Zion : and thou shalt see the good of Jerusalem all the days of thy life .
Psalm 120 : 1
A Song of degrees . In my distress I cried unto the LORD , and he heard me .

## October 12

Psalm 126 : 3
The LORD hath done great things for us ; whereof we are glad .
Psalm 121 : 7
The LORD shall preserve thee from all evil : he shall reserve thy soul .
Psalm 42 : 1
To the chief Musician , Maschil , for the sons of Korah . As the hart panteth after the water brooks , so panteth my soul after thee , O God .

Psalm 42 : 5

Why art thou cast down , O my soul ? Hope thou in God : for I shall yet praise him for the help of his countenance .

## October 13

Psalm 40 : 11

Withhold not thy tender mercies from me , O LORD : let thy lovingkindness and thy truth continually preserve me

Psalm 42 : 5

Many , O LORD my God , are thy wonderful works which thou hast done , and thy thoughts which are to us - ward : they cannot be reckoned up in order unto thee : if I would declare and speak of them , they are more than can be numbered .

Psalm 135 : 1

Praise ye the LORD . Praise ye the name of the LORD ; praise him , O ye servants of the LORD .

## October 14

Psalm 89 : 15

Blessed is the people that know the joyful sound : they shall walk , O LORD , in the light of thy countenance .

John 1 : 49

Nathanael answered and said unto him , Rabbi , thou art the Son of God ; thou art the King of Israel .

John 1 : 12

But as many as received him , to them gave he power to become the sons of God , even to them that believe on his name :

## October 15

Psalm 51 : 17 - 18

(17)The sacrifices of God are a broken spirit : a broken and a contrite heart , O God , thou wilt not despise .

(18)Do good pleasure unto Zion : build thou the walls of Jerusalem .

Psalm 128 : 2

For thou shalt eat the labour of thine hands: happy shalt thou be , and it shall be well with thee.

## October 16

Proverbs 17 : 22

A merry heart doeth good like a medicine : but a broken spirit drieth the bones .

Psalm 135 : 1

Praise ye the LORD . Praise ye the name of the LORD ; praise him , O ye servants of the LORD .

Psalm 135 : 14 -15

(14)For the LORD will judge his people , and he will repent himself concerning his servants .

(15)The idols of the heathen are silver and gold , the work of men's hands .

## October 17

Psalm 128 : 2

For thou shalt eat the labour of thine hands : happy shalt thou be , and it shall be well with thee.

Psalm 27 : 5 - 7

(5)For in the time of trouble he shall hide me in his pavilion : in the secret of his tabernacle shall he hide me ; he shall set me up upon a rock .

(6)And now shall mine head be lifted up above mine enemies round about me : therefore will I offer in his tabernacle sacrifices of joy ; I will sing praises unto the LORD .

(7)Hear , O LORD , when I cry with my voice : have mercy also upon me , and answer me .

## October 18

Psalm 27 : 4
One thing have I desired of the LORD , that will I seek after ; that I may dwell in the house of the Lord all the days of my life , to behold the beauty of the LORD , and to inquire in his temple .
Psalm 27 : 8
When thou saidst , Seek ye my face ; my heart said unto thee , Thy face , LORD , will I seek .
Psalm 27 : 4
One thing have I desired of the LORD , that will I seek after ; that I may dwell in the house of the LORD , all the days of my life , to behold the beauty of the LORD , and to inquire in his temple .

## October 19

Psalm 116 : 8
For thou hast delivered my soul form death , mine eyes from tears , and my feet from falling .
Psalm 135 : 4
For the LORD hath chosen Jacob unto himself , and Israel for his peculiar treasure .
Psalm 128 : 2
For thou shalt eat the labour of thine hands : happy shalt thou be , and it shall be well with thee.

## October 20

Psalm 104 : 31
The glory of the LORD shall endure for ever : the LORD shall

rejoice in his works .
Psalm 143: 10
Teach me to do thy will ; for thou art my God : thy spirit is good ;
lead me into the land of uprightness .

## October 21

Psalm 143 : 8
Cause me to hear thy lovingkindness in the morning ; for in thee
do I trust : cause me to know the way wherein I should walk ; for
I lift up my soul unto thee .
Psalm 27 : 11
Teach me thy way , O LORD , and lead me in a plain path ,
because of mine enemies .
Psalm 27 : 4
One thing have I desired of the LORD , that will I seek after ; that
I may dwell in the house of the LORD all the days of my life , to
behold the beauty of the LORD , and to inquire in his temple .

## October 22

Ezekiel 44 : 14
But I will make them keepers of the charge of the house ,
for all the service thereof , and for all that shall be done therein .
Psalm 119 : 105
NUN . Thy word is a lamp unto my feet , and a light unto my
path .

Psalm 40 : 13
Be pleased , O LORD , to deliver me : O LORD , make haste to help me .

Ecclesiastes 9 : 10 -11
(10)Whatsoever thy hand findeth to do , do it with thy might ; for there is no work , nor device , nor knowledge , nor wisdom , in the grave , whither thou goest .
(11)I returned , and saw under the sun , that the race is not to the swift , nor the battle to the strong , neither  yet bread to the wise , nor yet riches to men of understanding , nor yet favour to men of skill ; but time and chance happened to them all .
Psalm 23 : 5-6
(5)Thou preparest a table before me in the presence of mine enemies : thou anointest my head with oil ; my cup runneth over
(6)Surely goodness and mercy shall follow me all the days of my life : and I will swell in the house of the LORD for ever .

## October 24

Psalm 24 : 1
A Psalm of David . The earth is the LORD'S , and dthe fulness thereof ; the world , and they that dwell therein .
Psalm 134 : 1-3
(1)A Song of degrees . Behold , bless ye the LORD , all
ye servants of the LORD , which by night stand in the house of the LORD.
(2)Lift up your hands in the sanctuary , and bless the LORD .
(3)The LORD that made heaven and earth bless thee out of Zion .

## October 25

Psalm 128 : 2
For thou shalt eat the labour of thine hands : happy shalt thou be
, and it shalt be well with thee.
Psalm 17 : 15
As for me , I will behold thy face in righteousness : I shall be
satisfied , when I awake , with thy likeness .

## October 26

Psalm 19 : 7
The law of the LORD is perfect , converting the soul : the
testimony of the LORD is sure , making wise the simple .
Psalm 143 : 10
Teach me to do thy will ; for thou art my God : thy spirit is good ;
lead me into the land of uprightness .

## October 27

Psalm 140 : 12
I  know that the LORD will maintain the cause of the afflicted ,
and the right of the poor .
Psalm 128 : 2
For thou shalt eat the labour of thine hands : happy shalt
thou be , and it shall be well with thee.

## October 28

Psalm 87 : 1-3
(1)A Psalm or Song for the sons of Korah . His foundation is in
the holy mountain .
(2)The LORD loveth the gates of Zion more than all the

dwellings of Jacob .

(3)Glorious things are spoken of thee , O city of God .Selah .

Psalm 89 : 15

Blessed if the people that know the joyful sound : they shall walk , O LORD , in the light of thy countenance .

Psalm 73 : 24 - 25

(24)Thou shalt guide me with thy counsel , and afterward receive me to glory .

(25)Whom have I in heaven but thee ? And there is none upon earth that I desire beside thee.

## October 29

Psalm 40 : 1

To the chief Musician , A Psalm of David . I waited patiently for the LORD ; and he inclined unto me , and heard my cry .

Psalm 128 :2

For thou shalt eat the labour of thine hands : happy shalt thou be , and it shall be well with thee.

Psalm 86 : 2

Preserve my soul ; for I am holy : O thou my God , save thy servant that trusted in thee .

## October 30

Psalm 89 : 10

Thou hast broken Rahab in pieces , as one that is slain ; thou hast scattered thine enemies with thy strong arm.

Psalm 89 : 15

Blessed is the people that know the joyful sound : they shall walk , O LORD , in the light of thy countenance.

Psalm 128 : 2

For thou shalt eat the labour of thine hands : happy shalt thou be , and it shall be well with thee.

## October 31

Psalm 131 : 1-3

(1)A Song of degrees of David . LORD , my heart is not haughty , nor mine eyes lofty : neither do I exercise myself in great matters , or in things too high for me .

 (2)Surely I have behaved and quieted myself , as a child that is weaned of his mother : my soul is even as a weaned child .

(3)Let Israel hope in the LORD from henceforth and for ever .

Psalm 128 : 2

For thou shalt eat  the labour of thine hands: happy shalt thou be , and it shall be well with thee .

## November 1

Psalm 119 : 89
LAMED . For ever , O LORD , thy word is settled in heaven .
Psalm 128 : 2
Fore thou shalt eat the labour of thine hands : happy shalt thou be , and it shall be well with thee.

## November 2

Psalm 119 : 88
Quicken me after thy lovingkindness ; so shall I keep the testimony of thy mouth .
Psalm 7 : 9
Oh let the wickedness of the wicked come to an end ; but establish the just : for the righteous God trieth the hearts and reins .
Psalm 3 : 3
But  thou , O LORD , art a shield for me ; my glory , and the lifter up of mine head .

## November 3

Psalm 3 : 4
I cried unto the LORD with my voice , and he heard me out of his holy hill . Selah.
Psalm 128 : 2
For thou shalt eat the lanour of thine hands : happy shalt thou be , and it shall be well with thee .

## November 4

Psalm 107 : 22
And let them sacrifice the sacrifices of thanksgivings , and declare his works with rejoicing .
Psalm 107 : 1
O give thanks unto the LORD , for he is good : his mercy endureth for ever.
Psalm 134 : 1 - 3
(1)A Song of degrees. Behold , bless ye the LORD , all ye servants of the LORD , all ye servants of the LORD , which by night stand in the house of the LORD.
(2)Lift up your hands in the sanctuary , bless the LORD .
(3)The LORD that made heaven and earth bless thee out of Zion.

## November 5

Psalm 119 : 88
Quicken me after thy lovingkindness ; so shall I keep the testimony of thy mouth.
Psalm 135 : 5
For I know that the LORD is great , and that our Lord is above all gods.

## November 6

Psalm 106 : 5
That I may see the good of thy chosen , that I may rejoice in the gladness of thy nations , that I may glory with thine inheritance .
Psalm 117 : 1
O Praise the LORD , all ye nations : praise him , all ye people.

## November 7

Psalm 92 : 4
For thou , LORD , hast made me glad through thy work: I will triumph in the works of thy hands .
Psalm 119 : 16
I will delight myself in thy statutes : I will not forget thy word.
2 Chronicles 12 : 8
Nevertheless they shall be his servants ; that they may know my service , and the service of the kingdoms of the countries.
Psalm 37 : 28
For the LORD loveth judgement , and forsaketh not his saints ; they are preserved for ever : but the seed of the wicked shall be cut off.

## November 8

Psalm 37 : 30
The mouth of the righteous speaketh wisdom , and his tongue talked of judgement .
Psalm 37 : 29
The righteous shall inherit the land , and dwell therein for ever .
Psalm 40 : 1
To the chief Musician , A Psalm of David . I waited patiently for the LORD ; and he inclined unto me , and heard my cry .
Psalm 37 : 28
For the LORD loveth judgement , and forsaketh not his saints ; they are preserved for ever : but the seed of the wicked shall be cut off .

## November 9

Psalm 37 : 34
Wait on the LORD , and keep his way , and he shall exalt thee to inherit the land : when the wicked are cut off , thou shalt see it .

Psalm 134 : 1

A Song of degrees . Behold , bless ye the LORD , all ye servants of the LORD , which by night stand in the house of the LORD .

## November 10

Psalm 92 : 4

For thou, LORD , hast made me glad through thy work: I will triumph in the works of thy hands .

Psalm 51 : 17

The sacrifices of God are a broken spirit : a broken and contrite heart , O God , thou wilt not despise .

## November 11

Psalm 55 : 16

As for me , I will call upon God ; and the LORD shall save me .

Psalm 77 : 11

I will remember the works of the LORD : surely I will remember thy wonders of old .

## November 12

Psalm 78 : 1

Maschil of ASAP . Give ear , O my people , to my law : incline your ears to the words of mouth .

Psalm 49 : 1

To the chief Musician , A Psalm for the sons of Korah .

Hear this , all ye people ; give ear , all ye inhabitants of the world .

Psalm 55 : 16

As for me , I will call upon God ; and the LORD shall save me .

## November 13

Psalm 31 : 14
But I trusted in thee , O LORD : I said , Thou art my God.
Psalm 74 : 12
For God is my King of old , working salvation in the midst of the earth.

## November 14

Psalm 101 : 6
Mine eyes shall be upon the faithful of the land , that they may dwell with me : he that walketh in a perfect way , he shall serve me.
Psalm 117 : 1
O Praise the LORD , all ye nations : praise him , all ye people.

## November 15

Psalm 119 : 26 - 30
(26)I have declared my ways , and thou heardest me : teach me thy statutes .
(27)Make me to understand the way of thy precepts : so shall I talk of thy wondrous works .
(28)My soul melted for heaviness : strengthen thou me according unto thy word.
(29)Remove from me the way of lying : and grant me thy law graciously .
(30)I have chosen the way of truth : thy judgments have I laid before me .
Psalm 89 : 15
Blessed is the people that know the joyful sound : they shall walk

, O LORD , in the light of thy countenance.
Psalm 128 : 2
For thou shalt eat the labour of thine hands : happy shalt thou be
, and it shall be well with thee.

## November 16

Psalm 101 : 6
Mine eyes shall be upon the faithful of the land , that they may
dwell with me : he that walketh in a perfect way , he shall serve
me .
Psalm 89 : 15
Blessed is the people that know the joyful sound : thy shall walk ,
O LORD , in the light of thy countenance.

## November 17

Psalm 71 : 8
Let my mouth be filled with thy praise and with thy honour all
the day.
Psalm 73 : 17
Until I went into the sanctuary of God ; then understood I their
end.
Psalm 135 : 6
Whatsoever the LORD pleased , that did he in heaven , and in
earth , in the seas , and all deep places.

## November 18

Psalm 116 : 1
I love the LORD , because he hath heard my voice and my
supplications.
Psalm 143 : 6
I stretch forth my hands unto thee: my soul thirsteth after thee ,

as a thirsty land . Selah.

## November 19

Psalm 143 : 9 - 10
(9)Deliver me , O LORD , from mine enemies : I flee unto thee to hide me .
(10)Teach me to do thy will ; for thou art my God : thy spirit is good; lead me into the land of uprightness.
Psalm 128 : 2
For thou shalt eat the labour of thine hands : happy shalt thou be , and it shall be well with thee.

## November 20

Psalm 78 : 7
That they might set their hope in God , and not forget the works of God , but keep his commandments.
Psalm 71 : 1
In thee , O LORD , do I put my trust : let me never be put to confusion .
Psalm 55 : 16
As for me , I will call upon God ; and the LORD shall save me .
Psalm 85 : 1
To the chief Musician , A Psalm for the sons of Korah . LORD , thou hast been favourable unto thy land : thou hast brought back the captivity of Jacob.

## November 21

Psalm 84 : 12
O LORD of hosts , blessed is the man that trusted in thee.

Psalm 128 : 2

For thou shalt eat the labour of thine hands : happy shalt thou be ,and it shall be well with thee.

## November 22

Psalm 29 : 11

The LORD will give strength unto his people ; the LORD will bless his people with peace.

Psalm 27 : 4

One thing have I desired of the LORD , that will I seek after ; that I may dwell in the house of the LORD all the days of my life , to behold the beauty of the LORD , and to inquire in his temple.

Psalm 89 : 15

Blessed is the people that know the joyful sound : they shall walk , O LORD , in the light of thy countenance.

## November 23

Psalm 55 : 16

As for me , I will call upon God ; and the LORD shall save me.

Psalm 89 : 8 - 11

(8)O LORD God of hasts , who is a strong LORD like unto thee? Or to thy faithfulness round about thee?

(9)Thou rulest the raging og the sea : when the waves thereof arise , thou stillest them.

(10)Thou hast broken Rahab in pieces , as one that is slain ; thou hast scattered thine enemies with thy strong arm.

(11)The heavens are thine , the earth also is thine : as for the world and the fulness thereof , thou hast founded them.

## November 24

Psalm 86 : 5
For thou , Lord , art good ,and ready to forgive ; and plenteous in mercy unto all them that call upon thee.
Psalm 86 : 4
Rejoice the soul of thy servant : for unto thee , O Lord , do I lift up my soul.
Psalm 89 : 15
Blessed is the people that know the joyful sound : they shall walk , O LORD , in the light of thy countenance.
Psalm 89: 11
The heavens are thine , the earth also is thine : as for the world and the fulness thereof , thou hast founded them.

## November 25

Psalm 87 : 5
And of Zion it shall be said , This and that man was born in her :and the highest himself shall establish her .

Psalm 128 : 2
For thou shalt eat the labour of thine hands : happy shalt thou be , and it shall be well with thee.

## November 26

Psalm 23 : 5 -6
(5)Thou preparest a table before me in the presence of mine enemies : thou anointest my head with oil ; my cup runneth over.
(6)Surely goodness and mercy shall follow me all the days of my

life : and I will dwell in the house of the LORD for ever.
Psalm 78 : 7
That they might set their hope in God , and not forget the works of God , but keep his commandments:

## November 27

Psalms 64 : 7
But God shall shoot at them with an arrow ; suddenly shall they be wounded.
Psalm 65 : 1
To the chief Musician , A Psalm and Song of David . Praise waited for thee , O God , in Sion : and unto thee , shall the vow be performed .
Psalm 64 : 10
The righteous shall be glad in the LORD , and shall trust in him ; and all the upright in heart shall glory .
Psalm 128 : 2
For thou shalt eat the labour of thine hands : happy shalt thou be , and it shall be well with thee.

## November 28

Psalm 91 : 10 -11
(10)There shall no evil befall thee, neither shall any plague come nigh thy dwelling .
(11)For he shall give his angels charge over thee , to keep thee in all thy ways.
Psalm 89 : 28
My mercy will I keep for him for evermore , and my covenant shall stand fast with him.

Psalm 77 : 13
Thy way , O God , is in the sanctuary : who is so great a
God as our God ?
Psalm 78 : 7
That they might set their hope in God , and not forget the works
of God , but keep his commandments :

## November 29

Psalm 78 : 7
That they might set their hope in God , and not forget the works
of God , but keep his commandments.
I Corinthians 15 : 58
Therefore , my beloved brethren , be ye steadfast , unmovable ,
always abounding in the work of the Lord , forasmuch as ye
know that your labour is not in vain in the lord.

## November 30

John 14 : 16 - 17
(16)And I will pray the Father , and he shall give you another
Comforter , that he may abide with you for ever ;
(17)Even the Spirit of truth; whom the world cannot receive ,
because it seeth him not , neither knoweth him : but ye know
him ; for he dwelleth with you , and shall be in you .
John 15 : 16
Ye have not chosen me , but I have chosen you , and ordained
you , that ye should go and bring forth fruit , and that your fruit
should remain : that whatsoever ye shall ask of the Father in my
name , he may give it you .
Psalm 78 : 7
That they might set their hope in God , and not forget the works
of God , but keep his commandments.

## December 1

Psalm 78 : 12
Marvellous things did he in the sight of their fathers , in the land
of Egypt , in the field of Zoan.
Psalm 37 : 25
I have been young , and now am old ; yet have I not seen the
righteous forsaken , nor his seed begging bread .

## December 2

Psalm 39 : 12 -13
(12)Hear my prayer , O LORD , and give ear unto my cry ; hold
not thy peace at my tears : for I am a stranger with thee , and a
sojourer , as all my fathers were.
(13)O spare me , that I may recover strength , before I go hence ,
and be no more.
Psalm 64 : 10
The righteous shall be glad in the LORD , and shall trust in him ;
and all the upright in heart shall glory.
Psalm 11 : 1
To the chief Musician , A Psalm of David . In the LORD put I my
trust : how say ye to my soul , Flee as a bird to your mountain?

## December 3

Psalm 12 : 1
To the chief Musician upon Sheminith , A Psalm of David . Help
, LORD ; for the godly man ceaseth ; for the faithful fail from
among the children of men.
Psalm 71 : 1- 3
(1)In thee , O LORD , do I put my trust : let me never be put to
confusion

(2)Deliver me in thy righteousness , and cause me to escape : incline thine ear unto me , and save me.

(3)Be thou my strong habitation , whereunto I may continually resort : thou hast given commandment to save me ; for thou art my rock and my fortress .

Psalm 32 : 1

A Psalm of David , Maschil. Blessed is he whose transgression is forgiven , whose sin is covered.

## December 4

Psalm 31 : 24

Be of good courage , and he shall strengthen your heart , all ye that hope in the LORD.

Psalm 12 : 7

Thou shalt keep them , O LORD , thou shalt preserve them from this generation for ever.

## December 5

Psalm 17 : 15

As for me , I will behold thy face in righteousness : I shall be satisfied , when I awake , witty likeness.

Psalm 104 : 15

And wine that maketh glad the heart of man , and oil to make his face to shine , and bread which strengthen man's heart .

Psalm 103 : 1

A Psalms of David . Bless the LORD , O my soul : and all that is within me , bless his holy name.

## December 6

Psalm 102 : 12
But thou , O LORD , shalt endure for ever ; and thy remembrance unto all generations .
Psalm 103 : 2
Bless the LORD , O my soul , and forget not all his benefits :
Psalm 103 : 8
The LORD is merciful and gracious , slow to anger, and plenteous in mercy. Psalms 128 : 2
For thou shalt eat the labour of thine hands : happy shall thou be , and it shall be well with thee.

## December 7

Psalm 71 : 8
Let my mouth be filled with thy praise and with thy honour all the day.
Psalm 128 : 2
For thou shalt eat the labour of thine hands : happy shall thou be , and it shall be well with thee.

## December 8

Psalm 135 : 6
Whatsoever the LORD pleased , that did he in heaven , and in earth , in the seas , and all deep places .
Psalm 119 : 52
I remembered thy judgments of old , O LORD ; and have comforted myself.

I Kings 11 : 28

And the man Jeroboam was a mighty man of valour : and
Solomon seeing the young man that he was industrious , he
made him ruler over all the charge of the house of Joseph.

Psalm 73 : 24

Thou shalt guide me with thy counsel , and afterward receive me
to glory .

## December 9

Psalm 68 : 11

The Lord gave the word: great was the company of those that
published it.

Psalm 68 : 19

Blessed be the Lord , who daily loadeth us with benefits , even
the God of our salvation.

Ezekiel 11 : 19 - 20

(19)And I will give them one heart , and I will put a new spirit
within you ; and I will take the stony heart out of their flesh , and
will give them an heart of flesh :

(20)That they may walk in my statutes , and keep mine
ordinances , and do them : and they shall be my people , and I
will be their God.

## December 10

Ezekiel 11 : 19 -20

(19)And I will give them one heart , and I will put a new spirit
within you ; and I will take the stony heart out of their flesh , and
will give them an heart of flesh.

(20)That they may walk in my statutes , and keep mine
ordinances , and do them : and they shall be my people , and I
will be their God .

Psalm 73 : 24

Thou shalt guide me with thy counsel , and afterward receive me
to glory.

Psalm 74 : 12

For God is my King of old , working salvation in the midst of the earth .

Psalm 78 : 7

That they might set their hope in God , and forget the works of God , but keep his commandments :

Psalm 78 : 38 - 39

(38)But he , being full of compassion , forgave their iniquity , and destroyed them not : yea , many a time turned he his anger away , and did not stir up all his wrath.

(39)For he remembered that they were but flesh ; a wind that passeth away , and cometh not again.

## December 11

Psalm 8 : 6

Thou madest him to have dominion over the works of thy hands ; thou hast put all things under his feet:

Psalm 101 : 8

I will early destroy all the wicked of the land ; that I may cut off all wicked doers from the city of the LORD.

Psalm 78 : 7 -12

(7)That they might set their hope in God , and not forget the works of God , but keep his commandments :

(8)And might not be as their fathers , a stubborn and rebellious generation ; a generation that set not their heart aright , and whose spirit was not steadfast with God.

(9)The children of Ephraim , being armed , and carrying bows , turned back in the day of battle.

(10)They kept not the covenant of God , and refused to walk in his law ;

(11)And forgat his works , and his wonders that he had shewed them.

(12)Marvellous things did he in the sight of their fathers , in the land of Egypt , in the field of Zoan .

## December 12

Psalm 78 : 17
And they sinned yet more against him by provoking the most High in the wilderness .
Psalm 101 : 6
Mine eyes shall be upon the faithful of the land , that they may dwell with me : he that walketh in a perfect way , he shall serve me.
Psalm 77 : 1
To the chief Musician , to Jeduthun , A Psalm of Asaph . I cried unto God with my voice , even unto God with my voice ; and he gave ear unto me.

## December 13

Psalm 74 : 12
For God is my King of old , working salvation in the midst of the earth.
Psalm 135 : 1
Praise ye the LORD . Praise ye the name of the LORD ; praise him O ye servants of the LORD.

## December 14

Psalm 128 : 2
For thou shalt eat the labour of thine hands : happy shalt thou be , and it shall be well with thee.
Psalm 78 : 7
That they might set their hope in God , and not forget the works

of God , but keep his commandments :
Psalm 97 : 1
The LORD reigneth ; let the earth rejoice ; let the multitude of isles be glad thereof.
Psalm 102 :1A Prayer of the afflicted , when he is overwhelmed , and poureth out his complaint before the LORD. Hear my prayer , O LORD , and let my cry come unto thee.

## December 15

Psalm 110 : 1 -5
(1)A Psalm of David . The LORD said unto my Lord , Sit thou at my right hand , until I make thine enemies thy footstool .
(2)The LORD shall send the rod of thy strength out of Zion : rule thou in the midst of thine enemies.
(3)Thy people shall be willing in the day of thy power , in the beauties of holiness from the womb of the morning : thou hast the dew of thy youth.
(4)The LORD hath sworn , and will not repent , Thou art a priest for ever after the order of Melchizedek.
(5)The Lord at thy right hand shall strike through kings in the day of his wrath.
Psalm 97 : 1
The LORD reigneth ; let the earth rejoice ; let the multitude of isles be glad thereof.

## December 16

Psalm 62 : 1
To the chief Musician , to Jeduthun , A Psalm of David . Truly my soul waiteth upon God : from him cometh my salvation.

Psalm 60 : 5

That thy beloved may be delivered ; save with thy right hand ,
and hear me.

I Corinthians 3 : 6 -7

(6)I have planted , Apollos watered ; but God gave the increase.
(7)So then neither is he that planteth any thing , neither he that
watereth ; but God that giveth the increase .

## December 17

I Corinthians 4 : 2

Moreover it is required in stewards , that a man be found
faithful.

Jeremiah 1: 9

Then the LORD put forth his hand , and touched my mouth ,
And the LORD said unto me , Behold ,I have put my words in
thy mouth.

Psalm 31 : 24

Be of good courage , and he shall strengthen your heart , all ye
that hope in the LORD .

Psalm 27 : 4

One thing have I desired of the LORD , that will I seek after ; that
I may dwell in the house of the LORD all the days of my life , to
behold the beauty of the LORD , and to inquire in his temple.

## December 18

Psalm 27 : 11

Teach me thy way , O LORD , and lead me in a plain path ,
because of mine enemies.

Psalm 27 : 4

One thing have I desired of the LORD , that will I seek after ; that
I may dwell in the house of the LORD all the days of my life , to

behold the beauty of the LORD , and to inquire in his temple.
Psalm 28 : 2
Hear the voice of my supplications , when I cry unto thee , when I lift up my hands toward thy holy oracle .

## December 19

Psalm 97 : 1
The LORD reigneth ; let the earth rejoice ; let the multitude of isles be glad thereof .
Psalm 27 : 4
One thing have I desired of the LORD , that will I seek after ; that I may dwell in the house of the LORD all the days of my life , to behold the beauty of the LORD , and to inquire in his temple.

## December 20

Psalm 27 : 14
Wait on the LORD : be of good courage , and he shall strengthen thine  heart : wait , I say , on the LORD.
Psalm 27 : 13
I had fainted , unless I had believed to see the goodness of the LORD in the land of the living.
Psalm 84 : 12
O LORD of hosts, blessed is the man that trusted in thee.

## December 21

Psalm 59 : 17
Unto thee , O my strength , will I sing : for God is my defence , and the God of my mercy.

Psalm 97 : 1
The LORD reigneth ; let the earth rejoice ; let the multitude of isles be glad thereof.

## December 22

Psalm 71 : 8
Let my mouth be filled with thy praise and with thy honour all the day.
2 Chronicles 25 : 8
But if thou wilt go , do it , be strong for the battle : God shall make thee fall before the enemy : for God hath power to help , and to cast down.
2 Chronicles 14 : 11
And Asa cried unto the LORD his God , and said , LORD , it is nothing with thee to help , whether with many , or with them that have no power : help us , O LORD our God ; for we rest on thee , and in thy name we go against this multitude . O LORD , thou art our God ; let not man prevail against thee.
Psalm 40 : 1
To the chief Musician , A Psalm of David . I waited patiently for the LORD ; and he inclined unto me , and heard my cry.

## December 23

2 Chronicles 25 : 9
And Amaziah said to the man of god , But what shall we do for the hundred talents which I have given to the army of Israel ? And the man of God answered , The LORD is able to give thee much more than this.
Psalm 71 : 8
Let my mouth be filled with thy praise and with thy honour all the day.

Ezekiel 44 : 9 - 14

(9)Thus saith the Lord GOD ; No stranger , uncircumcised in heart , nor uncircumcised in flesh , shall enter into my sanctuary , of any stranger that is among the children of Israel .

(10)And the Levites that are gone away far from me , when Israel went astray , which went astray away from me after their idols ; they shall even bear their iniquity.

(11)Yet they shall be ministers in my sanctuary , having charge at the gates of the house , and ministering to the house : they shall slay the burnt offering and the sacrifice for the people , and they shall stand before them to minister unto them .

(12)Because they ministered unto them before their idols , and caused the house of Israel to fall into iniquity ; therefore have I lidded up mine hand against them , saith the Lord GOD , and they shall bear their iniquity .

(13)And they shall not come near unto me , to do the office of a priest unto me , nor to come near to any of my holy things , in the most holy place : but they shall bear their shame , and their abominations which they have committed .

(14)But I will make them keepers of the charge of the house , for all the service thereof , and for all that shall be done therein.

Psalm 128 : 2

For thou shalt eat the labour of thine hands : happy shalt thou be , and it shall be well with thee.

## December 24

Psalm 128 : 5

The LORD shall bless thee out of Zion : and thou shalt see the good of Jerusalem all the days of thy life.

Psalm 3 : 3

But thou , O LORD , art a shield for me ; my glory , and the lifter up of mine head.

## December 25

Psalm 11 : 4
The LORD is in his holy temple , the LORD'S throne is in heaven : his eyes behold , his eyelids try , the children of men .
Psalm 11 : 1
To the chief Musician , A Psalm of David . In the LORD put I my trust : how say ye to my soul , Flee as a bird to your mountain?
Psalm 68 : 19
Blessed be the Lord , who daily loadeth us with benefits , even the God of our salvation.

## December 26

Psalm 68 : 20
He that is our God is the God of salvation ; and unto GOD the Lord belong the issues from death .
Psalm 68 : 3
But let the righteous be glad ; let them rejoice before God : yea , let them exceedingly rejoice.
Psalm 67 : 1
To the chief Musician on Neginoth , A Psalm or Song . God be merciful unto us , and bless us ; and cause his face to shine upon us ; Selah.

## December 27

Psalm 66 : 1
To the chief Musician , A Song of Psalm . Make a joyful noise unto God , all ye lands :
Psalm 68 : 19
Blessed be the Lord , who daily loadeth us with benefits , even the God of salvation . Selah.

Psalm 100 : 3

Know ye that the LORD he is God : it is he that made us , and not we ourselves ; we are his people , and the sheep of his pasture.

Psalm 101 : 6

Mine eyes shall be upon the faithful of the land , that they may dwell with me : he that walketh in a perfect way , he shall serve me.

## December 28

Psalm 99 : 1-2

(1)The LORD reigneth ; let the people tremble : he sitteth between the cherubims ; let the earth be moved.

(2)The LORD is great in Zion ; and he is high above all the people.

Psalm 101 : 6

Mine eyes shall be upon the faithful of the land , that they may dwell with me : he that walketh in a perfect way , he shall serve me .

Psalm 101 : 1 -2

(1)A Psalm of David . I will sing of mercy and judgment : unto thee , O LORD , will I sing.

(2)I will behave myself wisely in a perfect way . O when wilt thou come unto me? I will walk within my house with  perfect heart.

## December 29

Psalm 68 : 20 -22

(20)He that is our God is the God  of salvation ; and unto GOD the Lord belong the issues from death.

(21)But God shall wound the head of his enemies , and the hairy scalp of such an one as goeth on still in his trespasses .

(22)The Lord said , I will bring again from Bashan , I will bring my people again from the depths of the sea .
Psalm 68 : 19
Blessed be the Lord , who daily loadeth us with benefits , even the God of our salvation. Selah.
Psalm 101 : 6
Mine eyes shall be upon the faithful of the land , that they may dwell with me : he that walketh in a perfect way , he shall serve me.

## December 30

Psalm 78 : 72
So he fed them according to the integrity of his heart ; and guided them by the skillfulness of his hands .
Psalm 128 : 2
For thou shalt eat the labour of thine hands : happy shalt thou be , and it shall be well with thee.

## December 31

Psalm 135 : 6
To him that stretched out the earth above the waters : for his mercy endureth for ever.

# A Years Journey

**J** - For his anger endureth but a moment : in his favour is life : weeping may endure for a night , but **joy** cometh in the morning

.

Psalm 30:5

**O** - For God so loved the world , that he gave his **only** begotten Son , that whosoever believeth in him should not perish , but have everlasting life.

John 3 : 16

**U** - He shall cover thee with his feathers , and **under** his wings shalt thou trust : his truth shall be thy shield and buckler.

Psalm 91 : 4

**R**- Create in me a clean heart , O God ; and **renew** a right spirit within me Psalms 51 : 10

**N** - O LORD our Lord , how excellent is thy **name** in all the earth.

Psalm 8 : 9

**E** - Though thy beginnings was small , yet thy latter **end** should greatly increase.

Job 8 : 7

**Y** - Howbeit when he , the Spirit of truth , is come , he will guide **you** into all truth : for he shall not speak of himself ; but whatsoever he shall hear , that shall he speak : and he will shew you things to come.

John 16 : 13

Spiritually Speaking and Walking with the Word of God

( A Years Journey)

**<u>Finally , my brethren , be strong in the Lord , and in the power of his might .</u>**

**<u>Ephesians 6 : 10</u>**

www.ingramcontent.com/pod-product-compliance
Lightning Source LLC
Chambersburg PA
CBHW081631040426
42449CB00014B/3255

9 780981 565842